THE AMERICAN GUIDE TO WINES

THE AMERICAN GUIDE TO

WINES

by Ruth Ellen Church

Introduction by Morrison Wood

FUNK & WAGNALLS • NEW YORK

Copyright © 1963 by Ruth Ellen Church
All Rights Reserved.

First paperbound edition published 1968 by Funk & Wagnalls

Published by arrangement with Quadrangle Books, Inc.

Printed in the United States of America

Photographs courtesy of THE CHICAGO TRIBUNE

5—73

ISBN 0-308-90074-X

For my Premier Grand Cru friends
ELIZABETH HEDGECOCK SPARKS
AND DOROTHY HOLLAND
companions in the wine cellars of France

CONTENTS

INTRODUCTION

Writing an introduction to a book by a dear friend and valued confrere is a hell of a job. If your praise is effulgent, you are biased. If you damn it with faint praise, you are being charitable. However, what follows is the absolutely unbiased and honest opinion of one who is not exactly unfamiliar with both wine and food.

For the average, ordinary individual who enjoys the pleasures of the table, Ruth Ellen Church has written a book on wines that, in my opinion, surpasses any other book of its kind. It is not tediously technical; its contents are not beyond the grasp of the normal mind or understanding; and it isn't "high hat" or sophisticated. It does, however, contain a wealth of information on the best known, and even less known, American and European wines that will enable the reader to have an excellent basic knowledge of wines (a better knowledge than the average wine dealer with whom he or she comes in contact), and to apply that knowledge to the end of a greater enjoyment of both wine and food.

In writing about wines there are two basic ways to approach the subject. One is from the point of view of the oenophile, the dedicated connoisseur and expert. The other is from the point of view of the amateur, the individual who knows little, or perhaps nothing, about wines, but who would like to enjoy them, either by themselves, and/or with food.

In a treatise on wines directed to the connoisseur and expert the writer will have evaluated wines solely on their vinous merits, bringing into play his sense of sight, his sense of smell and his sense of taste, all of which must be highly developed. He will discuss the color and clarity of a wine; its bouquet and aroma (its "nose"); its flavor, acidity, body and aftertaste; and its characteristics. He may compare it with other wines of its class; go into the matter of vintages; and discuss the grape from which it is made.

The amateur, however, wants to know things about wines that are rudimentary to the connoisseur. He wants to familiarize himself with the different classes and types of wines, and their characteristics. He wants to know how to select wines, and what the labels on wine bottles mean. He is particularly concerned about what wines go best with certain foods and dishes; what foods and dishes go best with certain wines. He wants to know how to serve wines, the temperatures at which various wines are at their best and the glassware in which they should be served. He wants to know how and where to store and keep the various wines. If he is interested in cooking, he wants to know how to best use wines to enhance the deliciousness of dishes. And finally, he wants to familiarize himself with the various wine terms.

In this book Ruth Ellen Church has skilfully woven together the two points of view, yet she is always writing for the amateur and answers all of his questions. And, incidentally, the expert may learn something from the chapter, "Wine Makes Food Taste Better."

This is much more than a wine primer. I would call it a wine guide book, because someone thoroughly familiar with the course is showing the way.

I have always thought that in order to write comprehensively and with authority about wine, one must have a wide knowledge of food and considerable experience in the preparation of food, because flavor, aroma and character are integral parts of both wine and food.

I don't believe that Ruth Ellen Church has a peer in the field of food and cooking. She is a graduate home economist, but I've never held that against her, because I've never known her to think or act or write like so many home economists who can be pretty dull when writing about food.

I have known Ruth Ellen for nearly twenty years. Since 1946 my weekly syndicated column on cooking, "For Men Only!" has appeared on her food pages in the *Chicago Tribune*, and during the ensuing years I have avidly read nearly everything Ruth Ellen and her highly capable staff have written about food and cooking.

Ruth Ellen Church approaches the business of preparing and cooking food with a spirit of inventiveness and a willingness to break with time-worn tradition. She feels that "what was good enough for Father" could be improved upon for his offspring. One doesn't find in her food pages and articles a drab procession of old, commonplace recipes, or the fancying-up of such recipes with nauseous additions.

At a time when the use of wine in recipes was frowned on by newspapers and magazines, Ruth Ellen would occasionally include a modicum of wine as an ingredient to make a dish more intriguing (thank God she never used those dirty words—"cooking sherry"). And, as bolder food writers began to ignore the ancient taboos and advocate the use of wine and spirits in cooking, Ruth Ellen happily joined the new trend. I vividly recall her recipe several years ago for an eggnog. It was potent and unbelievably delicious, and would make a Kentucky Colonel sit up and beg!

I don't know how or when the idea came to Ruth Ellen to write a book on wines. But I do know she approached her task with a thoroughness that characterizes everything she does. Researching the subject was not enough. Neither was visiting California and New York vineyards and talking extensively to vintners. On April 12, 1962, she sailed for Europe, and for more than two months she traveled around the great wine-producing areas of the European continent, tasting and evaluating wines, talking with vintners and cellar-masters, interviewing hundreds of wine men and gathering fascinating anecdotes on wines.

After Ruth Ellen Church wrote her wonderful book, *Magic Recipes for the Electric Blender*, I reviewed it in the *Chicago Sunday Tribune*. The burden of my song was: "It's fabulous, and ought to be in every home that has a blender as part of its kitchen equipment." Only recently I learned that the book is well on its way to the goal I mentioned, having sold nearly half a million copies to date.

As you've no doubt gathered by now, I think that *The American Guide to Wines* is fabulous also. It should be in the home of everyone who enjoys wine, or would like to enjoy wine.

I have a feeling in regard to goals that history will repeat itself.

MORRISON WOOD

Zurich, Switzerland

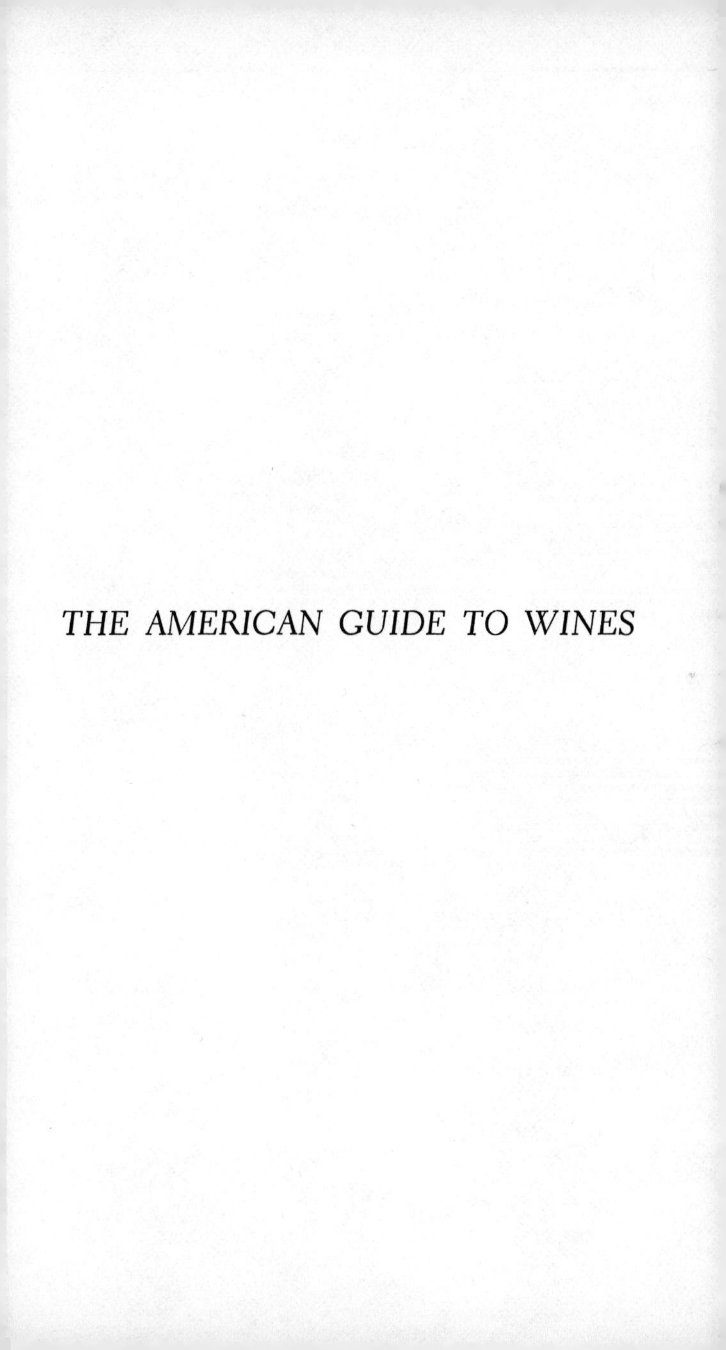

THE AMERICAN GUIDE TO WINES

1. AN INTRODUCTION TO WINES

A meal without wine, a day without sunshine.
–French aphorism

If Adam was the first man, he may also have been the first vintner.

Nobody knows just how wine was "invented," but there are many legends, just as there are legends relating to the origin of wine's boon companion, cheese. Both wine and cheese are natural foods; they didn't really have to be invented.

Nevertheless, there lived in ancient Persia, so the story goes, a king named Jemshid, who was exceedingly fond of grapes. He put some away in a jug once when he marched or galloped off to war, and by the time he arrived back home, the grapes were in turbulent ferment. So was one of his wives, who may have had reason to believe that she was no longer first in his affections.

Well, Jemshid ate or drank the grapes and developed an enormous tummy-ache (he probably had an enormous tummy to have it in—those old Persians were great eaters!). Blaming the jug of grapes, the king simply labeled them POISON (in Persian) instead of dumping them into the Caspian Sea. Some time later, the melancholy wife found the grapes, now completely turned to wine, and deciding to end it all, drank copious draughts from the jug.

She didn't die; she began to feel better. She laughed and danced and sang her way back into her husband's graces, whereupon they immediately began to live happily ever after (Jemshid is supposed to have lived 700 years; we do not know about the lady), making wine in the same way after every grape harvest.

The history of wine, not the legend, goes back to Egypt in 2400 B.C., but I have no intention of tracing the history of viticulture.

This is a practical book for everyday people who want to know how to buy, serve and enjoy wines. I am not a wine connoisseur—I was brought up on milk, as are most Americans. So I have acquired my wine knowledge the hard way, by digging it out, by visiting vineyards and wine cellars both here and abroad, by talking with connoisseurs, interviewing wine growers, asking questions of wine merchants. I think I have an advantage over some authors of books on wine who have always known about wines and who therefore don't realize how elemental is the knowledge of some of the most enthusiastic learners.

Americans are handicapped by not having a "past" in the area of viticulture. Grapes were first grown for wines in California less than two hundred years ago, and the years of prohibition were such a blow to the developing industry that only in the last few years has American winegrowing established itself firmly as an important part of our agriculture.

The development of the wine industry in California

especially has been phenomenal. American wines are now going abroad to compete in the marketplace with some of the classical wines of the world. Americans have a sudden thirst for knowledge about how to serve wines and build their own wine cellars. To the European, who has always drunk wine with his daily meals, wines are nothing new. They are new to us; they are exciting. They symbolize the ultimate in gracious living. But we don't know where to start in learning about wines. There seem to be too many rules and traditions, and too many wines!

This book will help you establish a good working base for wine scholarship and wine "know-how." It is a first reader, a reference book, a beginning.

Climb into my jeep with me and let's be off to the vineyards!

THE FIVE CLASSES OF WINES

A great light dawns on the amateur wine lover when he realizes that the thousands of labels on all the wines of the world can be stacked in just five piles. There are but five major classes of wines, with a number of basic types within each class.

I. APPETIZER WINES

Dry or cocktail Sherry and Vermouth are the leading examples. These wines, of 15 to 20 per cent alcoholic content, are served chilled before a meal. They also are good in the afternoon or evening with snacks.

II. WHITE TABLE WINES

Sauterne (So-*turn*), Chablis (*Shah*-blee), Rhine wine are examples of this class of 10 to 14 per cent alcohol wines.

They are usually dry (non-sweet), they are always served chilled and usually come to table with fish, poultry, eggs and light meats such as veal.

III. RED TABLE WINES

Burgundy, Claret and Chianti (Kee-*ahn*-tee) are in this group of dry red wines which are so good with beef and game. They also are popular companions of cheese. Alcoholic content is 10 to 14 per cent. These wines are served "at cool room temperature." They are not chilled.

Rosé (Ro-*zay*) wines, the pretty pinks, fit into the red table wine category but are something of an in-between. They are chilled, like white wines, to appear on the table, and they are as suitable for fish as for beef. Because of their versatility and wide appeal to wine amateurs, Rosés will be discussed in a section by themselves.

IV. DESSERT WINES

Port, Muscatel and sweet Sherry are good examples. These wines may be served with dessert, but sometimes come after it. They also may be served in mid-afternoon or evening. They have an alcoholic content of about 20 per cent. Most of them are strengthened with brandy. These wines keep well and usually are served at room temperature.

V. SPARKLING WINES

Champagne (Shahm-*pain*) is the star in this category. Sparkling Burgundy, sparkling Rosé and Italy's famous Asti Spumante (*Ahs*-tee Spoo-*mahn*-tee) are others. Usually these are considered festive wines, for special occasions. They are served chilled. Champagne and sparkling Rosé are good with all foods; sparkling Burgundy usually accompanies the meat course, and is sweeter than its non-bubbly brother. Asti Spumante is sweet; generally it is better with dessert or by itself. Alcoholic content of sparkling wines usually is 14 per cent or less.

HOW MANY SERVINGS IN A BOTTLE OF WINE?

It may not be very helpful to you to know that a tank car holds as much as 10,000 gallons of wine, a "pipe" 125 gallons or so, a butt 100 to 140 gallons and a barrel 50 gallons. I'm just throwing these figures in because they're the kind of thing you can toss at friends who are impressed by numbers. But here's some information in simpler arithmetic that you can use.

A "*split*" of Champagne or dinner wine contains 6 to 8 fluid ounces, and serves two with one glass each. Buy this size if you eat and drink alone, or if two of you want to drink a toast to celebrate your engagement or anniversary. Some winemakers are eliminating this size in favor of the "tenth."

A *half-bottle* or "*tenth*," 12 fluid ounces; two glasses for each of two of you. A half-bottle is a good choice for a twosome in a restaurant, especially when you are going to have more than one wine.

A *pint*, or 16 fluid ounces, provides four generous glassfuls.

A "*fifth*" (4/5 quart), holds 25.6 fluid ounces, and fills six glasses generously, eight glasses modestly.

A *quart* provides ½-cup portions for eight with its 32-ounce capacity. This means a half-filled 8-ounce wineglass, about standard for table wines.

Cheaper wines come in half-gallon and gallon jugs or

bottles. For special occasions Champagne may be bought in the magnum (52 ounces), and there are progressively larger sizes, rarely seen, known as Jeroboams, Tappit-hens, Rehoboams, Methuselahs, and so on up to the great-grand-pappy Nebuchadnezzar which probably neither you nor I shall ever see, and which holds over four gallons!

The servings suggested are for table wines only. Appetizer and dessert wines usually come in smaller portions, and therefore a bottle of Sherry or Muscatel would go about twice as far.

OF WINEGLASSES, BOTTLES, CORKSCREWS AND WINE CELLARS

JUST ONE GLASS FOR ALL WINES

The biggest favor the wine industry here and in France has done for consumers is to decide upon one all-purpose wineglass. Many American hostesses have been frightened away from wines, thinking they needed Sherry glasses, Champagne glasses and goblets for red and white wines in varying sizes. Few homes provide cupboard space; few pocketbooks can afford complete sets of glassware in many sizes.

And besides, it just doesn't make sense.

The all-purpose wineglass (see illustration) is a "tulip" shape of 8- or 9-ounce capacity and may be used for Sherry or dessert wines as well as for table wines. You just don't fill it so full. You don't fill it more than half-full for table wines, either, as you need "nose room" for catching that bouquet. The wine needs breathing space of its own, too.

I think that some wine publicists go too far in suggesting that wines may be drunk from jelly glasses or even paper cups—these take away all the charm. You can't see the color of a wine in a paper cup, a jelly glass is not crystal

The 8- or 9-ounce tulip-shaped all-purpose wineglass comes in inexpensive materials or in crystal, and is suitable for all kinds of wine, including Sherry, Champagne and dessert wines.

clear and has no stem. A stemmed glass lets you admire the wine and keeps your hand from cuddling and warming it (unless, of course, you *want* to cuddle and warm it, and you may, at times).

Colored glasses and decorated glasses interfere with the visual appreciation of a wine. Clear, clean, sparkling crystal is loveliest; but there are inexpensive glasses of good quality that do just fine.

The all-purpose glass is correct for Champagne, too, but another shape for Champagne glasses has been gaining favor, and it is available in moderately priced glassware. It is a taller, slimmer tulip, holding 7 ounces (you pour only 4 ounces of Champagne into it), and its chief advantage is that it has a narrowed surface and extended depth, so that Champagne will bubble longer in it than in the old-fashioned Champagne saucer. Hollow-stemmed Champagne glasses are not used much any more because they are hard to clean; for restaurant use in some states they are actually illegal.

Tiny Sherry glasses annoy wine connoisseurs. Complains one wine lover: "Those little glasses have to be filled full or you don't get a decent sized drink, and no wine glass should be filled full if you are to enjoy the wine's bouquet."

If you have Sherry glasses, use them for liqueurs, not Sherry. Put the Sherry in the all-purpose glass, the one you use for Burgundy or Rhine wine, Port and even Champagne.

THE SHAPE OF THE BOTTLE TELLS YOU THE KIND OF WINE—SOMETIMES!

Traditional bottles are used for most wines. There are some exceptions. Rosé bottles have no classical shape and the wine sometimes appears in unique containers. The pottery jug for Lancer's Crackling, the raffia lacework on the flat Lagosta (both of these are Portuguese wines) and the tall, tapered bottle, wide at the bottom, in which Provence's Château Ste. Roseline comes, are all distinctively different from any other bottles.

The highest quality Port and Sherry wines of Paul Masson in California are bottled in heart shapes. Several other wine producers pack all of their wines in one standard shape for economy and convenience.

However, you rarely see Champagne in anything but a Champagne bottle. A Champagne bottle is a large, heavy Burgundy bottle, one made to withstand the internal pressure of a bubbly wine.

The standard Burgundy bottle is dark green, stocky, with sloping shoulders and a long neck. California Bur-

Three traditional wine bottles are shown: from left, the Burgundy shape, holding the white Burgundy, Pouilly-Fuissé; the Rhine wine bottle, with a California Grey Riesling; and the dessert wine bottle, here used for Malmsey Madeira.

gundy types such as Pinot Noir (*Pea*-no Nwahr) and Gamay (Ga-*may*) come in this bottle as do France's famed Burgundies. The same shape in light-colored glass is used for white French Burgundies including Chablis, and for the domestic Chablis types.

Bordeaux wines and American Claret types come in a green bottle with nearly straight sides, curving shoulder and slender neck. This is sometimes called a "feminine" bottle as compared with the "masculine" Burgundy shape. California Cabernet Sauvignon (Cab-er-nay So-vee-nyohn) and Zinfandel (*Zin*-fan-dell) are bottled in it, being Claret types. A light-colored Claret bottle is used for Sauternes.

Almost anybody can recognize a Rhine wine by the tall, slender and graceful bottle which is traditional in Germany and here. Rhine wine and Rhine-type wines come in a brown bottle; Moselles and California Rieslings (*Rees*-lings) in the green Rhine wine bottle.

The Port bottle evolved through centuries from a squat jug to a straight-sided bottle with a toggle-shaped neck adapted to storage on its side without requiring much room. Port matures in the bottle, and sometimes space is a matter of great importance. The Port bottle has become the dessert wine bottle. It is made of brown glass for Port and Sherry, green for most other dessert wines.

The Italian *fiasco*, used for Chianti, has a round bottom, and is raffia wrapped and looped so that it may stand up or be suspended from a hook, if need be. This is certainly one of the most easily identified of all wine bottles.

AS FOR DECANTERS

The purpose of a decanter is to receive an old wine poured away from its sediment, usually after the bottle has lain for years in a wine cellar. You may never need one.

BOTTLES WITH CORKS REQUIRE A CORKSCREW

Many of our American wines come with easy-off metal caps. But high quality wines both here and abroad still come with corks—the better the wine, the longer the cork. Plastic stoppers would be more practical and could save much wine, but plastic stoppers aren't "romantic," and neither are the screw-on metal caps. We must have romance with at least some of our wines! Hence the need for a good corkscrew.

If you've been thinking of starting a corkscrew collection, don't, unless you are willing to look for years for an unusual one. Most of the really interesting corkscrews have already been gathered, many of them by Brother Timothy, cellarmaster of the Christian Brothers Winery in California. Brother Timothy has an assemblage of four hundred corkscrews from seventeen countries.

Another collector with years of experience and something to show for it is Irvin Padnos, proprietor of Chicago's Party Mart Wine Room.

Brother Timothy's most prized corkscrew is one made of a boar's tusk with a silver eagle's head, which also serves as a cigar cutter (see illustration). This one dates from the late 1700's. Then there's Andrew Volstead in effigy. Labeled "Old Snifter," Andrew hides his corkscrew under his coat. His nose and tie together make a bottle opener. Those who used the father of prohibition to open a wine bottle may have taken wry pleasure in putting "Old Snifter" to work in the wine cellar.

From Mr. Padnos' collection are shown "key to good cheer," a 7-inch auger-type cork extractor about forty-five years old; one with a hand-carved head of a German shepherd dog, made in Austria for a wine-lover whose dog had been killed by a wolf, and a silver pocket corkscrew of the type carried by gentlemen in the mid-1700's.

WHAT IS A GOOD PRACTICAL CORKSCREW?

A corkscrew that will pull a long cork without breaking or crumbling it and making you want to swear, should have a long "worm" without sharp edges, and the point of the worm should not be centered, but should be aligned with its spirals. It should have good leverage. Such a corkscrew can be very inexpensive. The one I like best has lever arms that project to either side of the bottle when the worm is firmly engaged. Press the arms with your two hands and the cork comes out surely and easily.

Cork extractors resembling hypodermic needles that operate by means of carbon dioxide cartridges have become quite popular. You insert the needle deep in the cork, press the proper spot on the handle and the cork is forced out by CO_2 released into the wine bottle. This extractor usually is very efficient, but it has its hazards. Now and then it pops a cork to the ceiling, producing a fountain of wine. One of my assistants opened a bottle of sparkling Rosé that way (a sparkling wine is already under pressure), and her family spent the evening washing walls and ceiling, curtains, cupboards, faces and hair! Theirs was the cleanest kitchen and the scrubbed-est family within miles! But only a taste of wine was left in the bottle!

Keep spare cartridges on hand for the cork extractor, or provide yourself with a good conventional corkscrew for the times when you run out of "juice."

A LITTLE WINE CELLAR UNDER THE SINK

If you have a cool (55 to 60 degrees) basement where it is dark, dry and quiet,* you have a perfect wine cellar. Go ahead and stock it with everything you can afford, including some rare Clarets to comfort you in your old age.

* Vibration is harmful to many wines. A motor for a home heating plant or even a washing machine can shake nearby shelves.

A sampling of antique corkscrews from two of the world's greatest collections–Brother Timothy of Christian Brothers and Irvin Padnos of Chicago.

Most wine lovers are happy to have a closet shelf or a spot under the sink amid the scouring pads in which to lay a few bottles of wine.

You can have a carpenter build you a wine "cellar" in a cupboard (perhaps you can do it yourself).

You can put a wooden, metal or plastic wine rack in any handy place which isn't near heating pipes and won't get too cold—70 degrees is too warm, and 35 degrees is too cold for wines.

Bottles with screw caps are stored standing up. They could be parked on a pantry shelf where it is dark and cool. Only the bottles with corks must be placed on their sides, to keep the corks wet. If corks dry out, the quality of the wine is impaired as the bottles are no longer airtight.

If you buy a case of wine, you can turn the case on its side and you'll have a wine rack to keep all the corks wet.

A bottle of Sherry, a bottle of Rosé and a bottle of dessert wine (if you like it cold) might be kept in your refrigerator ready for use. Since overchilling may cause sedimentation in the more delicate wines, it usually is better to chill for only an hour or two before serving. Try to avoid chilling again once the wine has warmed to room temperature.

Once you have your wine cellar, what are you going to put into it? A bottle of wine from each of the five basic wine groups will make you a good beginner's cellar. Replenish your stock as you use it and branch out in the red and white table wine categories as soon as you can. Start with a selection of California wines from the lists on pages 53 to 60. Or try an international selection.

INTERNATIONAL FIVE-BOTTLE BASIC WINE CELLAR

Appetizer Wine: A dry (fino [*feen*-oh]) Spanish Sherry may cost you nearly $5, but it is a good investment as it will last a long time and give you the assurance that you are serving the best to your guests.

White Table Wine: Buy a French Chablis, a Pouilly-Fuissé (*Pwee*-yee-Fwee-*say*) or a German Zeller Schwarze Katz, or Liebfraumilch.

Even a small apartment usually can accommodate a wine rack large enough to hold several kinds of wine. In the foreground of this picture are shown the favorite wine glasses of today: the tall, slim champagne, and the tulip-shaped all-purpose glass.

Red Table Wine: French Beaujolais (*Bo*-zho-lay) or California Cabernet Sauvignon.
Dessert Wine: Portuguese Port or Hungarian Tokay.
Sparkling Wine: California or New York state Champagne.

Morrison Wood, whose books on wine cookery are classics, suggests this more substantial wine cellar when young married couples ask him how to establish one.

24 BOTTLE CELLAR—$40 to $65

2 bottles California Grenache (Gren-*ahsh*) Rosé.
2 bottles California Cabernet Sauvignon (light, dry, red).
2 bottles California Pinot Noir (red, Burgundy type).
2 bottles California Riesling (German Rhine type, white).
2 bottles California dry Semillon (Say-me-*yohn*) (Sauterne type, white).
2 bottles California Pinot Blanc (white, Burgundy type).
2 bottles California Champagne (Korbel's is excellent).
1 bottle California brandy (Christian Brothers is excellent).
1 bottle California Port (Ficklin is excellent, when available).
1 bottle California dry Sherry (get premium quality).
1 bottle California sweet (cream) Sherry (get premium quality).
1 bottle French Burgundy.
1 bottle French white Burgundy.
1 bottle French Bordeaux, red.
1 bottle French Bordeaux, white.
1 bottle French Champagne.
1 bottle French Cognac.

The approximate cost for the above twenty-four-bottle cellar would be about $65. Omitting the fine imported items would bring the cost down to about $40.

KEEP A RECORD

A cellar book or record of the wines you have is important when you have acquired as many as a dozen bottles. Write down, under the basic five categories or a good system of your own:

The name of the wine and the vineyard.
The date purchased and the price.
The date removed from the cellar.
Your opinion of the wine after drinking it.

Such a record can be great fun. Some connoisseurs keep elaborate cellar books and include the labels from the bottles. But just a simple notebook will be helpful in getting started.

LOCK THE DOOR!

Keep your wine cellar locked. It holds your private treasure. Children should not have access.

"ROOM TEMPERATURE" IS 65 DEGREES!

How cold is "chilled," and how warm is "room temperature" in serving wines? Connoisseurs have written thousands of words to describe how much to chill the white wines that are to be served cold, and just how much to allow the red wines to warm after removal from the wine cellar.

All these discussions and sometimes obscure paragraphs may be cooked down to this: Chill the white table wines and Rosés for an hour or two; let the red wines "warm up" to around 65 degrees. If you keep your house at 72 degrees, *your* room temperature is a little warm for red wine. The term "room temperature" antedates modern heating! We need a new description for it.

Too cool is better than too warm, most authorities think. One may always warm the glass in the hand if the wine has been chilled so much that it refuses to release all of its bouquet.

Appetizer wines are served chilled and dessert wines may be chilled or not, as you like. Europeans don't chill their sweet wines, but Americans sometimes do. It's all a matter of taste.

TEMPERATURE EXTREMES ARE BAD FOR WINES

Most wines are fairly sturdy, but quality may be impaired if they are chilled and warmed too many times. Champagnes and vintage wines especially suffer from extremes of temperature. If you've chilled too many bottles of Champagne for a party, keep them cool—don't let them stand around at room temperature. If you have only a bottle or two left, refrigerate the wine and drink it within a reasonable time.

Jiggling is bad for old wines which should be "put to sleep" in a wine cellar and shouldn't be disturbed until you are ready to drink them. Vintage wines should be allowed to rest for a day or two after you carry them home from the wine shop before you open them.

WINE-TASTINGS ARE FUN

Amateurs and connoisseurs alike can enjoy a wine-tasting. The professionals, wine buyers and experienced tasters usually have extremely sensitive olfactory perceptiveness and intellectual taste buds, while those of us who are just plodding along acquiring our wine lore in bits and pieces have no such advantage. But do you know, I think we have more fun!

The experts sniff and swirl and taste and work hard

at appraising the body, aroma and bouquet (the professional nose, sniffing the wine, can isolate the grapes!). This wine has too much tannin; that one is "corky."

Happily, you and I smell, swirl, admire the color and fragrance, taste, and simply decide whether or not we like the wine. If we do, we make mental notes to serve it again.

As a food writer I am frequently invited to wine-tastings—of Italian red wines, French Burgundies, Swiss or Greek wines. These affairs are conducted fairly formally, and they sometimes are packed with wine buyers, society figures, wine lovers and occasionally with people just looking for free drinks who usually leave quickly when they discover that there is quite a difference between wine-tasting and having a drink. The practiced wine-taster first lifts the glass to the light to look for clarity and color; he then swirls the wine in the glass to increase the bouquet; then he smells, tastes and analyzes.

I have seen a wine importer simply smell and discard bottle after bottle of expensive wine because he did not consider it worthy to be presented at a tasting. I know of a French wine shipper who threw the staff of a large hotel into an uproar just before a wine-tasting because he insisted that all wineglasses be washed again—they tasted of detergent, he said. The professionals are exacting, as they need to be for our protection.

HAVE A WINE-TASTING PARTY

It is more fun to taste wine or present it on a smaller scale, at a party for one's friends, or more informally, for just one or two congenial wine lovers. The purpose of a wine-tasting is to make comparisons. Here are a few suggestions for a small but worthwhile wine-tasting.

1. Acquire as many Rosé wines as you can find or afford—a New York state Rosé, a Californian, a French, a Portuguese and an Italian. Present them chilled.

2. Try a group of Sherries or Vermouths, both domestics and imports, either dry or sweet. If you offer both dry and sweet, be sure to have the dry ones tasted first.

3. Prepare a tasting of dry red wines from as many different countries as possible, including a Chilean wine, one from Israel, Spain or Greece along with the more common Italian and French.

4. Collect a group of California wines, including Semillon, Sylvaner (*Sil*-vah-nur), Traminer (Trah-*meen*-er), Zinfandel, and compare them.

There are many other ways to go about having a wine-tasting; you can even do it with just two wines. It is sometimes more fun to conceal labels and just to number the bottles when comparisons are being made. A wine-tasting can be conducted like a popularity contest with ballots, or score sheets, if you wish.

Oftentimes the smaller the group and the less fuss made about it all, the more worthwhile the occasion is as a means of learning more about wine.

A young couple I know were invited to a "Hallowine" party on the 31st of October. Each couple brought a bottle of wine of a kind they enjoyed. All bottles were opened, tasted and compared. The couple who brought the best liked wine won a prize—a bottle of wine!

Cheese is wine's favorite companion—crackers or simple cookies to accompany the sweeter wines are sometimes offered at a wine-tasting, in addition, but more food dulls the impact of wine on the palate.

Glassware may be a problem. Few of us can provide enough glasses so that everyone may have a clean one for each wine sampled. But it usually is possible for each wine sipper to rinse his glass under the kitchen faucet between the Claret and the Burgundy or the Rhine wine and the Sauterne.

THE MARRIAGE OF WINE AND CHEESE

Had Omar Khayyam possessed a piece of cheese to eat with his loaf of bread and jug of wine, his paradise might have been "enow" without "thou."

Cheese is wine's perfect partner. The French speak of "the marriage" of wine and cheese and establish these three conditions:

1. Never serve cheese with a sweet wine.
2. Always serve red wine with cheese.
3. Any cheese will do, except cream cheese or goat milk cheese.

Happy-go-lucky Americans serve sweet wines with cheese. We also serve white wines with cheese, as do the Swiss and Germans, whose best wines are white. And if there's one thing we love, it's a good, gooey, oniony cream cheese dip with our wine!

Chacun a son gout.

Our lack of respect for tradition and the finer points of matching wines with cheese is painful to the French. I was sitting with a companion in a Paris restaurant which specializes in cheese—several hundred varieties, I think—and because we hadn't tried it, we ordered a Vouvray wine, perfectly conscious that by French standards we were making a mistake. Vouvray is a white wine, and somewhat sweet.

To compound the offense, we selected from the trays several soft, creamy, divinely delicious goat milk cheeses. We were soon conscious of a pair of mournful dark eyes looking our way from the next table. They belonged to a middle-aged, mustached man who seemed so disturbed by what he saw that he failed to hear the gay chatter of his pretty young luncheon partner. Before long he pushed back his chair, put his napkin by his plate, approached my companion and spoke. "Madame," he said, "you would like better the red wine!"

He was right, of course.

The French follow their meat and vegetables with wine and cheese, a good idea since the red wine served with the meat may be finished with the cheese. Those who wish to stop right there may skip the dessert that follows.

THE WINES FOR CHEESE

Red wines particularly suited to cheese include the Bordeaux and Burgundies, and American Clarets and Burgundies as well as the Cabernet Sauvignon and Pinot Noir wines which are as close to French Claret and Burgundy wines as we can come.

Beaujolais, Châteauneuf-du-Pape (Shot-oh-*nuf*-due-Pop), Barbaresco (Bar-bah-*rez*-coe), Valpolicella (Val-pol-lee-*cheh*-lah) and Chianti Classico are other particularly good choices.

THE CHEESES FOR WINE

There are dozens of possibilities, but these cheeses are choice, I think. Serve one or several.

Aged sharp cheddar, Fontina, Edam and Gouda
Swiss, Gruyere, Brick, Muenster, Monterey Jack
Brie, Camembert, Port du Salut
Roquefort, Blue and Bleu, Gorgonzola

The blue-mold cheeses should have robust wine companions, such as Burgundy or a high quality Chianti. Or possibly dry Sherry.

Sharp cheese spreads are good with wine.

When you wish to serve cheese with a Swiss or German white wine, why not settle on Swiss or gruyere?

Whatever combinations of wine and cheese suit your palate are probably the perfect "marriages" at your house.

2. WHAT ARE THE RULES?

When you ask one friend to dine, give him your best wine!
When you ask two, the second best will do.
–Henry Wadsworth Longfellow

The American host and hostess, newly interested in serving wines, are sometimes confused by the connoisseurs who lay down firm rules, and the eager beavers who want so much to sell more wine that they'd toss all the niceties out of the window.

There is a middle ground between the narrow rules of the pros and the no-rules of the pushers. It helps to realize that the "correct" thing is usually the most natural, comfortable and logical procedure. But one with little experience needs some guide lines:

SEVEN PRINCIPLES OF WINE SERVING

1. White table wines* usually accompany fish, seafood and light meats including turkey, chicken and veal.
2. Red table wines usually are served with roast beef, steaks, other beef cuts, lamb, pork, venison and game birds.
3. Dry (non-sweet) wines are served before sweet ones.
4. Light-bodied wines are served before full-bodied wines.
5. White table wines are served before red ones.
6. Rosé wines and Champagne may be served at any time of day and throughout a meal.
7. Red table wines and dessert wines should be served at cool room temperature; white wines and Rosés should be chilled. Appetizer wines such as cocktail Sherry and Vermouth are better chilled or on the rocks; cream or sweet Sherry usually is served at room temperature.

These are general customs wherever wine is drunk, simply because they represent what pleases most palates most.

Room temperature seems to be better for red wines, especially old red wines, because the aroma flowers with warmth. Chilling the wine inhibits the bouquet. Fine red wines need to be uncorked an hour ahead of serving time so that air and the warmth of the room may allow the bouquet to expand. Like a kitten let out of a cage, the wine unfolds, stretches comfortably and even seems to purr!

* "Table" or "dinner" wines are the non-sweet ones served with food.

THE ETIQUETTE OF WINE SERVING

Seldom is more than one wine served with a meal. The use of several wines suggests an important dinner or a banquet. One might serve cocktail Sherry or Vermouth as an appetizer, however, then follow with a Burgundy or Claret for the beef, and later offer Port or Muscatel in the living room after the meal. Thus there would be three wines, but only one would be served at the table.

In wine-drinking countries there would be no water glass, but on American tables there usually is one at each place. The water glass goes directly above the knife, and the wineglass to the right of it, usually a little closer to the diner. If there are two wineglasses, one for red and one for white wine, they may be lined up horizontally with the water glass, or more usual, make a right angle, with red wine glass to the right of the water glass, white wine glass below that. The empty wineglass is always removed from the table before the other one is filled.

It is usual for the host to pour the wines, and it is customary for him to pour a little into his own glass first, and to try it for approval before serving guests. A servant at home or a waiter in a restaurant will pour a little wine into the host's glass first and wait for his nod before going around the table clockwise, filling the women's glasses first, and returning to the host to pour a fuller glass.

There used to be more reason than politeness for this practice. In those "olden days," the host bravely made sure the wine was not poisoned! Now he just wants to make certain it is good wine, or the wine he ordered. If there are any bits of cork in the wine, he's the one who will get them.

Wineglasses are not lifted from the table when wine is poured. A slight twist of the wrist in lifting the bottle will hold the drop that otherwise might spot the tablecloth. There are silver wine-pouring tops for wine bottles that will not permit a drop to fall in the wrong place. These make nice gifts for wine-loving friends.

It is considered proper to allow guests to see the label of the wine bottle. To wrap the bottle with a napkin is a bit sneaky—as though you're ashamed of the wine!

TIPS ON OPENING THE BOTTLE

Have a good corkscrew ready (see page 26). Cut the foil neatly below the lip of the bottle. Don't just rip it off. Wipe the mouth of the bottle, uncork the wine and then wipe the mouth of the bottle once more. Then you are ready to pour.

HOW ABOUT COCKTAILS? CIGARETTES?

The Wine and Food Society and other associations of gourmets and wine lovers lay down firm rules: no cocktails; no smokes before a dinner with wines. After a few cocktails it is impossible to appreciate fine wine and good food. Smoking dulls the palate. These are the reasons given for the no martini, no cigarette rule (smoking is permissible *after* dinner).

But Americans do not give up their bad habits easily. For martini lovers and smokers, here are two comforting thoughts: It has been determined, I know not how, that *one* martini before dinner will not greatly reduce your appreciation for the wine. And the flavor of Sherry (but only Sherry) reaches right through to you even with a cigarette in your other hand, and smoke on your tongue!

To do honor to a fine wine, one should certainly present an unsullied palate, but for everyday meals with everyday wines, the cocktail and smoking questions will have individual answers. In other words, do as you like!

When two wines are served with a meal, the glasses may form a right angle with the water glass. The glass for white wine, usually served first, is closest to the diner. The second wine, usually red, is poured after the first glass has been removed from the table.

NO WINE WITH THE SALAD?

A vinegary dressing kills the taste of wine. That's the reason for the common caution, "Never serve wine with a salad." It's good advice, but has its exceptions. Chicken salad and seafood salads, dressed with mayonnaise instead of vinegar and oil, taste wonderful accompanied with a Rhine wine, Chablis or Rosé!

A WINE BASKET ON THE TABLE?

Why not? I wouldn't pay any attention to those fussy wine fanciers who proclaim that wine baskets and cradles are only for bringing rare old wines from the cellar without shaking them up!

Bird baths are for the birds, too, but your patio party will be praised if you fill *your* bird bath with cracked ice and use it to chill the Champagne! Why be stuffy?

WHAT ARE THE BEST VINTAGES?

Why don't you stop worrying about vintages? They're highly overrated.

Ninety-three per cent of the wines we drink are American wines. *American wines are not vintage wines.* There's a saying that the grapes *always* ripen in California. This is true, on the whole, and since every year is a good year, it is not necessary to set apart any year's produce with a date. The few dated domestic wines are mostly for show, although there are a select few that will age,* and these do have a reason for carrying a year on the label.

Of the imports, Sherry and Champagne are blended

* Pinot Noir and Cabernet Sauvignon from the better vineyards.

wines. They have no vintage years (a very few Champagnes for connoisseurs do carry vintage dates).

Only about 5 per cent of the wines we drink are vintage wines. They include the great Clarets of Bordeaux and the Burgundies and Rhine wines.

Vintages are mentioned in the chapters on Burgundy and Bordeaux. Even here it is easy to go astray, for a "great" year in one area may not have been a great year in another. Vintage charts usually reflect one man's opinion and seldom do two vintage charts agree. If you are going to buy a vintage wine, go to a reliable wine dealer and accept his advice.

Otherwise, forget about vintages until your postgraduate course in wines—then let us hope you have a well-padded wallet to pay for your great wines!

3. THE WINES OF CALIFORNIA

My manner of living is plain and I do not mean to be put out of it. A glass of wine and a bit of mutton are always ready, and such as are content to partake of that are always welcome. Those who expect more will be disappointed.—*George Washington*

After dinner, in George Washington's time, it was customary to drink thirteen toasts, one to each new colony. Had the father of his country possessed clairvoyance, there might have been a fourteenth toast to a future member of the union, 3,000 miles away, then successfully growing grapes for wine.

The new nation's colonists had been trying unsuccessfully to grow European grapes. Their wines were Sherry, Port and Madeira, and sometimes they could obtain Claret and Rhine wine.

They were temperate men, these early Americans, and wines were to them both food and medicine.

Across the wilderness of mountains, valleys, forests and rivers, Spanish missionaries were successfully growing grapes for wines in California. Father Junipero Serra is said to have planted the first grapes in 1769. Those grapes, appropriately enough, were called mission grapes, and they still are used today in the production of dessert wines.

The real father of California's wine industry, however, was not a monk growing wines for the glory of God, but a political refugee from Hungary who came to California in the gold rush days, stopping en route long enough to found the town of Sauk City, Wisconsin. He was Count Agoston Haraszthy, and he later spent two years in Europe gathering 100,000 cuttings from three hundred varieties of Europe's finest grapes. These were transplanted to California soils best adapted for them, and most of them flourished.

California's pride is a wine named *Zinfandel,* from cuttings brought by Haraszthy which cannot be traced. There appears to be no other red wine like it in the world today.

Count Haraszthy led a stormy life and was always in some kind of political or other hot water. He fled California in 1868 and is thought to have met his Maker between the jaws of a crocodile in Nicaragua in 1869.

California has not forgotten its debt to him. A big and beautiful book, *The Story of Wine in California** was dedicated to him in 1962.

From all of the finest winegrowing regions of Europe came settlers who brought with them not only vines but the practices and traditions of their regions, to add to the developing wine industry in California.

There were setbacks. A severe one was the phylloxera devastation of the 1890's that hit California vineyards after ruining those of Europe over a period of thirty years. Phylloxera, a root-killing louse, was the black plague of vineyards; it wiped out Burgundy and Bordeaux, rampaged

* University of California Press. Text by M. F. K. Fisher, photographs by Max Yavno.

through Switzerland, Germany, Italy, Spain and Portugal, then hopped to California in the 1890's to do its evil work.

Ironically, the root louse was taken to Europe on some eastern American vine cuttings. Grape varieties which are native to our eastern states can carry the pest without succumbing to phylloxera, but the European grapes, which are the kinds also grown in California, are not resistant. The results of this little experiment with American vines were cataclysmic.

Eventually the cure was found to be "hair of the dog." Europe's vineyards, and California's too, were re-established by grafting the vines onto phylloxera-resistant *roots* from the U.S. Thus, European wines are grown on American roots, and New York has a toehold in California vineyards!

Some years after phylloxera, along came prohibition, a tragic era in California winegrowing regions. And in between, there was the San Francisco earthquake. The vineyards that survived prohibition were those which were permitted to make sacramental wines, or those which turned to grape juice and jam. Some made a "grape concentrate." Could they help it if their customers added water and yeast and stirred up something in the basement washtub?

But thousands of acres of vineyard went to ruin, and the winemaking equipment with them. It is a miracle that California's wine industry has emerged so healthy and skillful that the rest of the world watches with keen interest and is beginning to buy the wines!

To the blessings of nature, soil and climate for the culture of hundreds of the world's best grape varieties, has been added the technology for constant development and improvement of vines and winemaking. Much of the research is done on the Davis Campus of the University of California under the direction of Professor Maynard Amerine, one of the world's authorities on wines and vines.

New hybrids that produce wines quite different from

Europe's classic types are being developed at Davis, and winemakers are eager for them. Emerald Riesling is one of the hybrids. It is being made into a varietal wine with fresh, tart flavor by Paul Masson Vineyards.

Individual winegrowers are always trying something new: new grape varieties, new equipment, new techniques. One interesting project in the Livermore Valley wineries of Cresta Blanca is the cultivation of Europe's "noble mold," the *botrytis cinerea*, a fungus which blesses the grapes it infects, producing precious, rare, sweet wine. Small quantities of Cresta Blanca Premier Semillon are the result. When available, this wine is expensive.

CALIFORNIA'S NINE WINE DISTRICTS

The nine wine districts of California stretch 700 miles from Mt. Shasta almost to Mexico, covering nearly a half-million acres. The best wines, the red and white table wines and some excellent Champagnes, come from the northern coastal counties. The hot interior regions are good for the development of grapes used to make sweet wines—still the greatest production, but gradually giving a few points to the table wines as the American taste slowly changes from sweet to less sweet, and from less sweet to dry.

By far the largest production from all regions is that of "standard" mass-produced wines. They are good wines, because California has strict laws to regulate their production and protect the consumer. They are O.K. for everyday drinking, and they are cheap. For the most part, they are blends of whatever grapes are handy.

Names of the bulk producers are familiar—Gallo, Petri, Italian Swiss Colony, Roma. Some of these companies are innovators of new types of wine. Gallo, for example, has created a battery of aperitif wines (fortified)

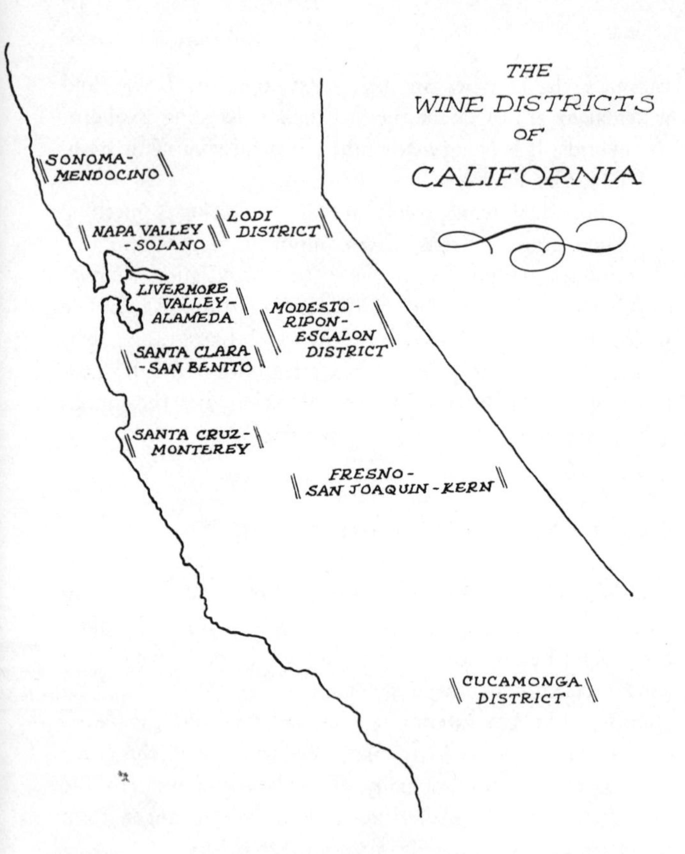

which are good for mixed drinks or "on the rocks" and seem to please the popular taste. About forty companies now are making them. They are called "natural flavor" wines, because they have to be that, legally. The flavors may include lemon and other fruits, herbs and spices—even chocolate! These drinks are known by such names as "Thunderbird," "Gypsy Rose" and "Ripple."

Geographically, California is divided into three wine-growing *regions*: the northern coastal region, home of the finest table wines and top quality Champagnes; the hot inland valley region, where dessert wines and bulk-fermented

Champagnes are made; and the warm southern California region, which makes aperitif and dessert wines, also table wines and Champagne.

These regions include the nine districts:

Northern Coastal (top quality table wines)	Sonoma—Mendocino Napa Valley—Solano Livermore Valley—Alameda Santa Clara—San Benito Santa Cruz—Monterey
Inland Valley (dessert wines, bulk Champagne)	Lodi Modesto—Ripon—Escalon Fresno—San Joaquin—Kern
Southern California (all kinds of wine)	Cucamonga

HOW WINE IS MADE

A billion bottles of wine come from California each year, and the state furnishes 85 per cent of the wines America drinks.

The winemaking process varies with the wine being made and the winegrower. But this is it, in brief:

1. Grapes are crushed and juice drawn off (red wines are fermented with their skins and pulp).

2. Juice ferments, usually in large vats. Sometimes yeast is added to promote the fermentation.

3. Fermentation is halted before all of the grape-sugar converts to alcohol, unless a very dry wine is wanted. Complete fermentation usually results in a wine of 10 to 14 per cent alcohol, a dinner wine. For Port, Sherry and Muscatel, fermentation is arrested with brandy at the desired stage of sweetness.

4. The fermented wine is aged in casks for months or years, depending upon the kind of wine and the quality it is to have. During aging it accumulates sediment and must be "racked" or drawn off the lees periodically.

5. Aging smooths and mellows the wine. When aging has perfected the wine, it is filtered and bottled.

6. After bottling, the wine usually is aged for several months or a year or two.

This brief treatment indicates nothing of the time and care required during these processes. Correct temperatures and storage conditions are important. Many factors operate to influence the quality of the wine on its way from grape to consumer.

VISIT THE WINERIES

Winery tours are week-end fun for Californians. When you vacation there, do spend half a day or more visiting a winery. Most companies welcome tourists; some of the bigger ones conduct tours every day of the week. Many of the settings are incredibly beautiful, and you'll be able to see vineyards, fermentation rooms, aging cellars and bottling processes. Particularly fascinating are the procedures for Sherry and Champagne, but you should see table wine made first.

Most tours wind up with a wine-tasting, and it is often possible to purchase at the winery unusual wines which do not go into general distribution. At the St. Helena wineries of Louis Martini, for example, people in the know scramble for an effervescent muscat wine known as Moscato Amabile, a delicate, sweet dessert wine in the Champagne bottle. It must be kept chilled until it is drunk, as its light 7 per cent alcohol content doesn't preserve it with the bubbles.

READ THE LABEL!

You can learn a lot about California wines (and others) by reading the labels. The front label gives you the basic information—the name of the wine, who makes it and where, the alcoholic content and possibly something more. But the back label may tell you the story of the wine, and is quite likely to offer some serving suggestions. Some people collect labels and paste them in scrapbooks, adding comments about the wine for future guidance. Soaking the empty bottle in hot water is sometimes a successful way of removing the label, but some of the glues now used in labeling are mighty resistant. However, it occasionally is possible to wheedle the wine producer out of a set of labels that haven't been pasted.

GENERICS AND VARIETALS

Generic names in California include Sauterne (without the French final *s*), Rhine wine and Chablis in white table wines; reds include Burgundy, Claret and Italian. These are "types" of wines, very loose classifications. They are blends of a number of wines made from various grapes, and most are ordinary though some may be very good.

If you want to try California's best, buy the *varietal* wines, those named for the grapes that go into them, instead of for European prototypes. French wines known as Burgundy or Chablis or Sauternes may be made only in legally limited areas in France and from specific varieties of grapes. A wine made a mile from the boundaries of the Sauternes district, even though from the identical grapes, may not presume to call itself Sauternes. But in California the name has been appropriated for a raft of white wines bearing no resemblance to the French wine and not made from the sauternes grapes at all. The same thing is true of the Burgundies, Clarets, "Rhine wines" and Chiantis* of California.

To carry the name of a grape, a California wine must be made of at least 51 per cent of the juices of that grape. The better varietals are made 85 to 100 per cent from the grape which names them.

Varietal wines are proud of their grapes, and the region which grows them. In addition to the name, *Cabernet Sauvignon,* for example, the wine label states the region, say Napa, or Sonoma. The vineyard name is the third guarantee of quality on the label, and possibly the best one.

THE WHITE TABLE WINES OF CALIFORNIA

White wines are the fish wines, and California offers a great variety. The best white table wines come from the northern coastal counties in the vicinity of San Francisco, where there is plenty of sun and plenty of rain with the "coolth" that is favorable for growing grapes such as the sauvignon blanc, chardonnay and riesling.

Most white wines are made from light-colored grapes, although a few, including French and some California Champagnes, include some blue-black grapes such as the pinot noir, with skins removed to keep the wine white.

California's white table wines range from very dry to rather sweet. All are served cold but not icy, at somewhere around 50 degrees, or as cold as one or two hours in the refrigerator will make them. If they are too cold, flavor and fragrance do not blossom as they should.

Following are the common generic names in California white table wines. Opposite appear names of some of the varietals, which, remember, are named for their grapes. Varietals are the superior wines.

* Chianti has its imitators even in Italy. French laws are far more strict.

When California grapes are ripe, no time is lost. They are picked at once, loaded in trucks, and taken to the crushing sheds which usually are a part of the wineries.

GENERIC NAME *(Type of Wine)*	VARIETAL NAME *(Named for grapes)*
Sauterne (So-*turn*)	Sauvignon Blanc (So-vee-nyon Blahn) Semillon (Say-me-*yohn*), dry or sweet
Rhine wine or Riesling (*Rees*-ling)	Grey Riesling Johannisberg Riesling (Yo-*hann*-is-burg) White Riesling Sylvaner (*Sil*-vah-nur) Traminer (Trah-*meen*-er) and Gewürztraminer (Geh-*wurtz*-trah-*meen*-er)
Chablis (white Burgundy)	Chardonnay or Pinot Chardonnay (*Pea*-no Shar-doh-*nay*) Chenin Blanc (*She*-nin Blahn) Folle Blanche (Fohl *Blahnsh*) Pinot Blanc

THE SAUTERNES

California Sauternes never are as sweet as their French counterparts, but they range from semi-sweet to dry.* The sweeter ones will be labeled "haut" (pronounced *oh*), "sweet" or "chateau" Sauterne. These wines are golden, full-bodied and fragrant. The better wines in this category will be made from one or both of the French sauternes grapes, the sauvignon blanc or the semillon. Sauvignon Blanc is fuller bodied and may be more aromatic than semillon. The best of the latter comes from the Livermore Valley.

The sweet Semillons and Sauvignons Blancs, as well as sweet "Sauterne," may be served with pastry, soufflé or fruit at the end of a meal, as well as with fish, seafoods and light meats such as veal and chicken.

* There's no such thing as a dry French Sauternes. These wines are all extremely sweet and luscious. The "noble rot" is responsible.

THE RHINE WINES

German Rhine wines are made from the riesling grape, but if you want a California wine from this grape, you must ask for *Johannisberg Riesling,* or *White Riesling.* These two are the same grape. Many authorities favor calling the grape and the wine White Riesling to avoid confusion with the imported wines from Germany and Switzerland known as Johannisberg.

Rhine wines and the varietals in this classification are light-bodied and very dry. *Traminer* is next best after Johannisberg or White Riesling. Sometimes this is called "Gewürztraminer." *Sylvaner* is a varietal made from a popular German and Alsatian grape, less aristocratic than the others. It is a pleasing wine, however, and has an alternative name, *Franken Riesling.*

Grey Riesling is not a true riesling grape, but the wine is soft, spicy and easy to like. It is currently very popular in social circles in the San Francisco Bay area.

Emerald Riesling, a hybrid grape developed at the University of California, makes a very pleasing white wine of that name.

THE CHABLIS

Wines in this category are fruitier than Rhine wines and less tart. Chablis is a white Burgundy of France, and may be produced only in a legally defined area around the village of Chablis, and from the pinot chardonnay grape. California *Pinot Chardonnay* is therefore its only real varietal; this wine is also called simply *Chardonnay.* Bottled by one of the prominent growers, this would be an exceptionally fine wine.

Pinot Blanc is a varietal of the Chablis type next in quality to the Chardonnay. It is fragrant and fresh, and best when it comes from the Livermore, Napa and Santa Clara valleys.

Folle Blanche is a wine made from what in France are known as cognac grapes. Cognac wines are not very good wines,* but they make wonderful cognac. In California the folle blanche grape makes a better wine than it does in France. It is so dry as to be tart, fresh and fruity.

Chenin Blanc is a varietal made from a grape of the Loire valley in France. It resembles Vouvray (*Voov*-ray) more than Chablis and is a pleasant white wine.

White wines, whether generic or varietal, are good companions not only for fish and seafood, but for turkey, chicken, veal, lamb, omelets, egg and cheese dishes, cold cuts, macaroni and cheese, rice and cheese and many light luncheon dishes.

CALIFORNIA WHITE VARIETAL WINES AND SOME OF THEIR VINEYARDS

Those resembling Sauternes

Sauvignon Blanc: Almadén, Beaulieu, Christian Brothers, Concannon, Cresta Blanca, Charles Krug (a sweet wine), Wente Brothers.

Semillon (*dry*): Almadén, Buena Vista, Christian Brothers, Cresta Blanca, Charles Krug, Louis M. Martini, Weibel, Wente Brothers.

Semillon (*sweet*): Christian Brothers, Cresta Blanca, Inglenook, Charles Krug, Wente.

(Château Beaulieu, Château Novitiate,† Château Masson, Château Wente and the Premier Semillon of Cresta Blanca are considered superior to other Semillons by the producers. These are the Semillons closest to the sweet Sauternes of France.)

* While visiting the region I was told, "Only the peasants drink them."
† From Novitiate of Los Gatos.

Those resembling Rhine wines

Emerald Riesling: Paul Masson. (The grape is a hybrid developed at the University of California. Masson calls the wine "Emerald Dry.")

Grey Riesling: Almadén, Buena Vista, Christian Brothers, Cresta Blanca, Charles Krug, Weibel, Wente.

Johannisberg or White Riesling: Almadén, Beaulieu, Buena Vista, Christian Brothers, Charles Krug, Louis M. Martini, Souverain Cellars.

Sylvaner: Almadén, Buena Vista, Christian Brothers, Concannon ("Riesling"), Inglenook ("Riesling"), Charles Krug, Louis M. Martini (Mountain Sylvaner), Souverain Cellars (Franken Riesling).

Traminer: Almadén, Buena Vista, Inglenook, Charles Krug, Louis M. Martini (Gewürztraminer).

Those resembling Chablis

Chardonnay or Pinot Chardonnay: Almadén, Beaulieu, Buena Vista, Christian Brothers, Cresta Blanca, Inglenook, Charles Krug, Paul Masson, Weibel, Wente.

Chenin Blanc: Charles Krug, Louis M. Martini.

White Pinot: Christian Brothers, Charles Krug, Louis M. Martini, Inglenook, Souverain Cellars.
(This wine resembles French Vouvray more than Chablis; it is light and fruity, dry or semi-dry, sometimes sweet.)

Folle Blanche: Louis M. Martini.

Pinot Blanc: Almadén, Weibel, Wente.

The wineries which produce these varietal white wines in almost every case also produce good generics, blended wines they market as Sauterne or Rhine wine or Chablis, selling at lower prices. Some of the varietals carry a vintage year.

An interesting comparison can be made of the same wine produced in different vineyards. There'll be surprises!

THE RED TABLE WINES OF CALIFORNIA

California red table wines, like other red wines of the world, are made from red, blue-black or purple grapes, fermented with their skins.

Top quality red wines of California, like top quality whites, come from the northern coastal counties and are varietal wines, named for their grapes.

They are wines to accompany meats and game at dinner and to serve with cheese at any time. The best of them (Cabernet Sauvignon or Pinot Noir) will age well.

Open the bottle half an hour to an hour before mealtime to let the wine "breathe" if it is one of the really good ones. Cool room temperature is right for serving.

GENERIC NAME (*Type of Wine*)	VARIETAL NAME (*Named for Grapes*)
Burgundy	Pinot Noir (*Pea*-no Nwahr) Gamay or Gamay Beaujolais (*Bo*-zho-lay)
Claret	Cabernet Sauvignon Zinfandel
Italian	Barbera (Bar-*beh*-rah) Grignolino (Green-yo-*leen*-oh)

THE BURGUNDIES

The noble grape of Burgundy is the pinot noir. If you buy a California wine with that name, you are buying the best "Burgundy" California makes. Pinot Noir from a top vineyard will grow better in the bottle. You may keep it in your wine cellar six or eight years or longer, if conditions are right. Most pinot noir wines are not 100 per cent varietals because the grape is difficult to grow and a poor yielder. But an 85-per-cent pinot noir with the other portion in gamay is a very fine wine indeed.

Gamay and *Gamay Beaujolais* are lighter, fruity wines comparable to France's Beaujolais, from lower Burgundy. They are gay, happy, informal wines, best cold, some think. They don't usually age well.

THE CLARETS

Cabernet Sauvignon is probably California's best wine. From the better vineyards of the northern hills and valleys it can be of such quality that it will age gracefully in your home wine cellar for ten years or more. The grape is the true Bordeaux grape, but in California it produces different wine, of course. It is wine that often can match quality with some of France's better Clarets.

Zinfandel is a California exclusive, since it can't be traced to any other winegrowing region of the world. The best of it comes from the colder winegrowing regions of the north of California. It has been compared with the Beaujolais of France, but is lighter-bodied, so that it better fits the Claret category.

ITALIAN TYPES

Barbera is made from a grape native to the Piedmont region of Italy. In California it produces a tart, full-bodied, beautiful red wine perfect to sip with Italian foods and other well-seasoned dishes.

Grignolino is a grape which produces good red wines in northern Italy and some of the best red and Rosé wines of California. The fragrance is said to be that of strawberries. The color is light, with an orange tone.

OTHER CALIFORNIA REDS

California *Chianti* is usually sold in the typical straw-covered round-bottomed bottle. It is a generic type, made of a blend of red wines. It usually is ruby red, medium tart, medium full-bodied and just the thing for pizza or spaghetti.

Vino Rosso is a generalized term for mellow red wines which are slightly sweet and usually carry Italian names.

CALIFORNIA RED VARIETAL WINES AND SOME OF THEIR VINEYARDS

Those resembling Burgundy

Gamay or Gamay Beaujolais: Christian Brothers, Inglenook, Charles Krug, Paul Masson.

Pinot Noir: Almadén, Beaulieu, Buena Vista, Christian Brothers, Cresta Blanca, Inglenook, Charles Krug, Louis M. Martini, Paul Masson, Weibel.

Those resembling Claret

Cabernet Sauvignon: Almadén, Beaulieu, Buena Vista, Concannon, Christian Brothers, Inglenook, Charles Krug, Paul Masson, Louis M. Martini, Souverain Cellars, Weibel.

Zinfandel: Buena Vista, Charles Krug, Cucamonga Winery, Louis M. Martini, Souverain Cellars.

Italian types

Barbera: Cucamonga Winery, Louis M. Martini.

Grignolino: Cucamonga Winery.

The vineyards named also produce generic types of wine and in many cases a full line of wines including Champagnes, Sherry, Port and Vermouth.

4. NEW YORK AND OTHER AMERICAN WINES

Wine is a constant proof that God loves us and loves to see us happy.—Benjamin Franklin

THE WINES OF NEW YORK STATE

Some of our country's most interesting wines come from the state of New York. They are truly American wines, not copies of anything that Europe has given to the world. Catawba, Niagara, Delaware, Elvira, Concord—grapes such as these are natives. They are of the *vitis labrusca* species, whereas California's grapes are from the European *vitis vinifera* vines. If you want to make a New York state winegrower see red, speak of these wines as having a "foxy" taste. They are different, all right—fresh tasting, earthy perhaps, fruity and possibly a little "wild." Therein lies their charm. Foxy or not, their very unlikeness to other wines is part of their fascination.

The Finger Lakes district of upper New York is their home, Lakes Keuka and Canandaigua in particular. These long, lovely lakes in the foothills of the Alleghenies are bordered by stony hillsides perfect for grape-growing. The area has been compared to the Rhine valley and to the Champagne district of France. White wines and Champagnes are New York's very best. The Taylor Wine Company of Hammondsport, on Lake Keuka, is the largest Champagne producer in the United States and one of the largest in the world.

When Leif Ericson and his Vikings discovered America in 1000 A.D., they found wild grapes growing in profusion and called this new land "Vineland the Good." European settlers later tried to make wines from these wild grapes and to plant their own vitis vinifera, and failed in both undertakings. It wasn't until the late 1700's that the rampant wild grapes were tamed and crossbred sufficiently for winemaking. The first vines were planted in the Finger Lakes area in 1830.

One of the early hazards to imported grape vines was phylloxera, the infamous root louse which we have already mentioned as ravaging the vineyards of Europe and California. Vitis labrusca vines can be a "Typhoid Mary," carrying the peril to other vines while firmly retaining an immunity from the lousy disease. Because of this immunity, labrusca and related species are the foundation for vineyards all over the world. European grapes will grow on these strong roots without changing character.

The riesling grape is the only vinifera variety that now grows in the East, but many hybrid vines with French parentage are being grown, and these promise a good many new and interesting wines in the future. It is very likely that they will retain the characteristic ("foxy"?) aroma and taste of the eastern grape.

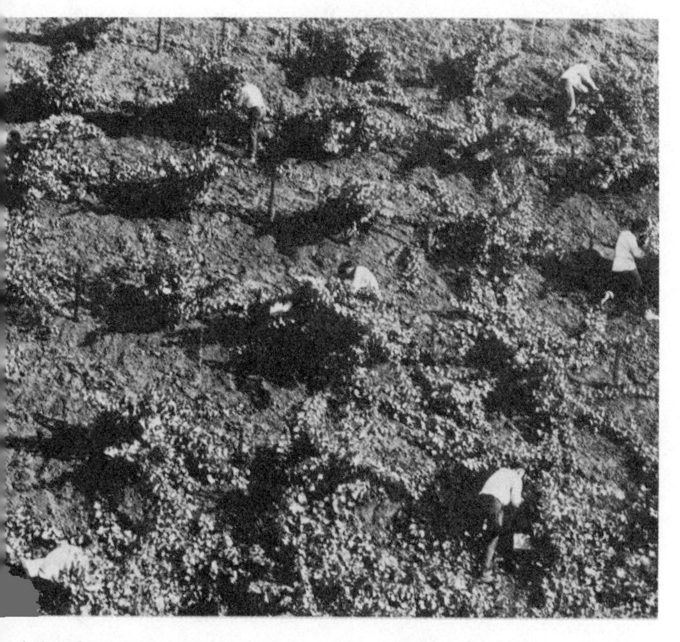

A hard rain or a high wind can ruin a vineyard when the grapes are ripe. Wine men keep an eagle eye on the weather and field workers must "make hay" while the sun shines. Many hands are needed to harvest the grapes quickly.

Most eastern wines have sugar added. The long days of sunshine in California allow grapes to develop their own sugars, but in the East summers are short, and grapes remain acid. Sugar doesn't necessarily mean sweeter wine; it is possible to ferment it all into alcohol. Sugar is simply necessary for the process of fermentation. So are yeasts, in eastern wineries. They are specially grown yeast cultures of which the vintners are proud.

THE BIG THREE WINEGROWERS OF THE FINGER LAKES

The Taylor Wine Company in 1962 purchased the Pleasant Valley Wine Company, its Lake Keuka neighbor, and thereby added the Great Western label to its line. The resulting assortment of wines pretty well covers the wine cellar. There are sweet and dry Vermouths, dry, medium and sweet Sherries, ruby, white and tawny Ports, Tokay, Claret, Burgundy, Rhine wine, Chablis, Sauterne, Rosé. Of the collective Champagnes, the most popular is "brut" (very dry). Another favorite is the Taylor pink Champagne. There is also a sparkling Burgundy in the line. Taylor and Great Western Muscatels are made from muscat wine shipped in from California.

Taylor wines are blended and standardized in quality. They are not labeled as to year; such a date would be meaningless. Except for the sparkling wines the caps are the easy-off kind Americans seem to prefer. Corks are not used.

Widmer's Wine Cellars at Naples, on Lake Canandaigua, has more of the old world approach to winemaking than Taylor, the modern mass-producer. Widmer's makes many varietal wines. They are 100 per cent varietals, even though legally a wine may be a varietal if it is made with 51 per cent of the juices of the grape it is named for.

Widmer's varietals include Catawba, Lake Niagara,

Grapes grown for fine wines require old world care at harvest time. Hand picking assures quality and perfect ripeness in the fruit of the vine. These grapes come from a vineyard in the Finger Lakes district of New York.

Delaware, Elvira, Moore's Diamond, Dutchess and others. They are dated, for as a company officer explains, "New York, like Europe, has years of good and poor vintage." In a 100 per cent varietal wine, this may make some difference. Widmer's has also been able to grow the riesling grape and produce a Riesling wine—there have even been several "auslese" (*aus*-selected, *lese*-picking) years, when the wine has been made of selected bunches of "noble mold" touched grapes. Seibel-Rosé, made from a French hybrid, is a distinctly different, assertive pink wine. It would be interesting to compare it in a tasting with a Grenache Rosé from California. The varietal wines are cork-sealed.

Widmer is proud of its five Sherries which age in white oak casks on the roof of the winery for four years (eight years for the special selection Sherry). The company is also proud of having produced a cocktail Sherry very Spanish in character without the flor yeast of Spanish Sherry, which will not develop in the New York climate.

This company also offers Rhine wine, Haut Sauternes (with the *s*, as spelled in France), Port, "Widmerheimer" red and white wines, brut Champagne, pink Champagne and sparkling Burgundy. There is also a Muscatel from eastern grapes.

Widmer managed to stay in business during prohibition by making quantities of Concord grape juice, jam and sacramental wines.

The third Finger Lakes winegrower of importance is Gold Seal Vineyards, Inc., also at Hammondsport, on southern slopes bordering Lake Keuka.

Gold Seal is famous for its Champagnes and specializes in them. The company even has a European subsidiary directed by Col. Peter Townsend, the man who didn't marry the Princess Margaret. Col. Townsend purchases wines which Gold Seal imports and distributes under the Maxim's label. Gold Seal New York wines are not sold in France. It's a one-way current.

A banquet given for Queen Elizabeth on her visit to Chicago a few years ago featured Charles Fournier Brut Champagne, the top-drawer Champagne from Gold Seal Vineyards. There are many who acclaim this premium Champagne as best in the United States. It is named for the man who "created" it, Charles Fournier, Gold Seal president, who was formerly general manager of a famous French Champagne firm, Veuve Cliquot, in Rheims.

Other Champagnes in the line include Gold Seal brut, extra dry, pink Champagne and sparkling Burgundy. Fournier Nature is "dry white wine for the connoisseur." It is a Champagne without the usual "dosage" of sweetening, a difficult wine to make.

Gold Seal offers some generics as well as Champagnes: Rhine wine, Claret, Burgundy, Rosé, Sauternes and "dry" Sauternes. Sherry and Port are also produced under the Gold Seal label.

Varietals include Delaware, a pale, straw-colored dry wine, Catawba and pink Catawba, both sweet dessert wines. Tokay and Concord wines are other sweet ones.

THOSE NEW YORK CHAMPAGNES

While New York State Champagnes are made by the French method (see page 133), they are made of other grapes—New York grapes such as Catawba and Delaware, plus some of the newer French hybrids, rather than pinot noir and chardonnay which will not grow in eastern soil and climate.

Great Western label (Taylor) Champagne requires seven wines of various ages in its blend, I was told when I visited there. Pink Champagne takes five white wines and two reds, sparkling Burgundy five reds and two whites.

The characteristic flavor of eastern grapes is absent from the Champagnes.

OHIO WINES AND MESSRS. LONGWORTH AND LONGFELLOW

"The day is not distant when the Ohio River will rival the Rhine in the quantity and quality of this wine. . . . It rivals the best Hock and makes a superior Champagne."

This prediction was made in 1845 by millionaire wine hobbyist Nicholas Longworth, grandfather of the Nicholas Longworth who was "Teddy" Roosevelt's son-in-law and for many years speaker of the House of Representatives.

The wine which held such promise was a sparkling Catawba developed by Longworth, so famous that Longworth once issued an indignant public charge that certain New York hotels were trying to pass off French Champagne as the elegant and distinguished Cincinnati Catawba!

Mr. Longworth sent a few bottles of his wine to the poet Henry Wadsworth Longfellow, impelling the famous author of Evangeline and Hiawatha to spout some verse which, while no match for the immortal lines of Thackeray in praise of bouillabaisse, or those of Ogden Nash in dispraise of salad, have become an enduring part of the history of American wines.

A modern day Catawba (not sparkling), produced by Gold Seal Vineyards in New York, even back-labels the last four lines as well as the familiar first quatrain:

> Very good in its way is the Verzenay
> Or the Sillery, soft and creamy.
> But Catawba wine has a taste more divine,
> More dulcet, delicious and dreamy.
> There grows no vine, by the haunted Rhine.
> By the Danube or Guadalquiver,
> Nor island or cape that bears such a grape
> As grows by the beautiful River.

(Verzenay and Sillery are French Champagnes; Guadalquiver rhymes with river, if you haven't studied Spanish.)

The Ohio river hasn't lived up to Longworth's dream, and no completely dulcet and dreamy Catawba wine exists today. But the state of Ohio produces some very good wines, and the Catawba is their grape.

The grape-growing, winemaking region of Ohio has shifted from the Cincinnati area cross-state north and east to Sandusky and the small islands in Lake Erie, where the water tempers the climate to protect vines from early budding and late frost. Scattered on the islands and along the shoreline are numerous wineries, the largest and most important of which is Meier's Wine Cellars.

Meier's sparkling Catawba wines now are called Champagne. They are made by the "charmat" or bulk fermentation method wherein the secondary fermentation is carried on in large tanks rather than bottles. Few Champagne lovers know the difference, and the charmat process makes possible more uniform and cheaper wines.

The company produces a Lake Erie sweet Catawba wine and some non-alcoholic still and bubbly Catawba juices. The customary Sherries, Ports, Vermouth and Muscatel are included in Meier's well-rounded lineup, but table wines are their pride. Isle St. George Sauterne, sweet and semi-sweet; Lake Erie Islands Rhine wine; Lake Erie white Burgundy (Chablis type); red Burgundy; Claret and Rosé are the important table wines.

All of these wines, it should be remembered, are made from native American grapes (Catawba and several others) which are very unlike European and California grapes and produce wines of completely different character. Aroma and flavor have been called "a little wild"—indeed, they have been called "foxy," too, and I don't think the term is opprobrious. They are unusual wines, carefully made, all-American, and well worth cultivating.

A list of other wine producers of the Sandusky area will be found on pages 266 and 267.

5. THE WINES OF FRANCE

Only a fool would deliberately go through life without Claret.
–S. S. Field, in the "American Drink Book."

If all the paeans of praise for French wines which have been sung for several thousand years could be piled upon each other, they would reach to outer space and sink France to the bottom of the Atlantic. French wines are those by which the wines of all other countries are judged and usually found lacking.

But it is important for us to remember that the really great French wines represent a very small percentage of the wines of the world and even of France. The everyday wines of France are no better than good California wines; some of them are not as good.

The great wines of France are usually very expensive, and they are wines for banquets and special occasions. One does not drink a Château Margaux (Mar-go), a Montrachet (*Moan*-rah-shay) or a Romanée Conti (Rome-ah-*nay* Kawn-*tee*) of a great year just any old time. France does, however, send us a good many excellent wines of lesser pedigree, well within reach of a wine enthusiast's pocketbook.

The two great wine districts of France are Bordeaux and Burgundy. In any argument about which wines are better, there never can be a winner. It is a matter of personal taste. A French woman who is internationally known for cooking, and who is herself owner of vineyards in other districts, tells me this: "When my husband and I were younger, we preferred Burgundy. Now that we are in our fifties, Bordeaux wines have more appeal—Burgundy is too *strong* for us." Burgundies are robust wines; the Clarets of Bordeaux are lighter, softer. But few of us will want to limit our wine preference to one or the other of these famous kinds of wine. We may wish to suit the wine to the food it accompanies to the table, a Burgundy with a magnificent roast or with venison, for example, and a Claret with filet mignon, if we can afford that meat. I have eaten dinner in French homes where several wines were served, and both a Bordeaux and a Burgundy appeared at the same meal.

Champagne is the wine of the third great French wine district. It is discussed in Chapter 8.

There are lesser districts where famous French wines are produced. The valley of the Loire, the Rhône Valley, Provence, from whence come the lovely pink wines of the Mediterranean area, and Alsace, home of white wines which are more German in character than French. In Alsace the wines are named for the vine—Riesling, Gewürztraminer (considered best), Sylvaner. Elsewhere in France the name of the wine is the name of its place of origin.

"Appellation Controlée," or control of names, is a rigidly enforced system in France. This is the way it works:

Wines made anywhere in the Bordeaux region (legally defined) may call themselves Bordeaux wines. The same is true of Burgundy and the other regions.

Within the Bordeaux area a further breakdown gives a district name to a wine: Graves (Grahv), St. Émilion (San-teh-mee-lee-*awn*), etc. In Burgundy the next classification might be Côte de Nuits (Coat duh *Nwee*). Drawing the lines closer, a Graves wine may be known by its vineyard name, such as Château Haut-Brion (Oh-Bree-*awn*). A Côte de Nuits town, Gevrey-Chambertin (*Zhev*-ray-*Shahm*-ber-tahn), lends its name to Burgundies produced within its legally limned borders, but there is a final breakdown here to the vineyard. Le Chambertin is the ultimate aristocrat of Gevrey-Chambertin.

The more specific the appellation, the greater the wine, and the costlier, too!

A typical label from a bottle of French wine (in this case, a château-bottled Bordeaux), illustrating the various terms explained in this chapter.

THE WINE REGIONS OF FRANCE

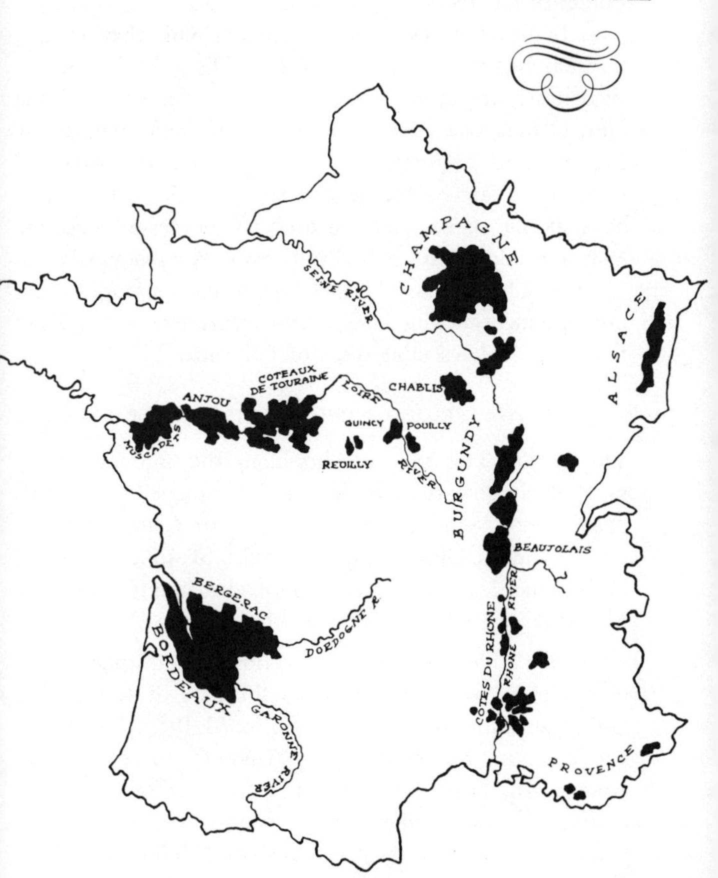

THE WINES OF BORDEAUX

With 2,000 years of experience behind her, how could Bordeaux fail to be a great wine grower?

Bordeaux wines are red, white and pink; they are dry, medium-dry, sweet and very sweet. There is a wine for every taste, for every dish. Bordeaux is the home of the great Clarets, claret being the English simplification of the French word "clairette," an old term for red wines of Bordeaux. Claret is the general term; all the better wines have specific names and the everyday Bordeaux wines are known as Bordeaux, not Claret. Still, everybody talks of "French Clarets," and "Claret" has been appropriated for use on American wine labels encircling American red wines that somewhat resemble those of Bordeaux.

THE FIVE PRINCIPAL WINE DISTRICTS OF BORDEAUX

The Medoc: This area stretches along the Gironde estuary into which flow the Garonne and Dordogne rivers. The "haut-medoc" produces most of the great Clarets. Famous village names include Margaux, Moulis, St. Julien, Pauillac, St. Estephe. The wines are red, light-bodied and fragrant. The Medoc is by far the largest-producing district.

St. Émilion: The wines from this small district are the oldest in France, dating back to the days of Rome. The last great Latin poet, Ausonius, praised the wines of St. Émilion, and himself owned a vineyard there. Château Ausone still bears his name. The St. Émilion wines are more robust than those of the Medoc—they're a red wine "for red meat," being deep-toned and full-bodied. One famous name from St. Émilion is Château Cheval Blanc.

Pomerol: Pomerol is a tiny district next to St. Émilion. The wines are red, also robust, but slightly lighter than those of St. Émilion. Château Pétrus is a Pomerol wine.

THE WINE REGIONS OF BORDEAUX

GIRONDE
MEDOC
HAUT MEDOC
ST. ESTEPHE
PAUILLAC
ST. JULIEN
MARGAUX
CÔTES DE BLAYE
CÔTES DE BOURG
POMEROL
ST. EMILION
DORDOGNE RIVER
BORDEAUX
ENTRE-DEUX-MERS
STE. FOY BORDEAUX
GRAVES
GARONNE RIVER
BARSAC
SAUTERNES

Graves: Gravelly soil gives Graves its name. The wines are both red and white. The red ones are fruity, the white dry to medium-dry, delicate yet "vigorous."

Sauternes: Sauternes includes the township of Barsac. Wines from this district are golden, sweet and mellow. They are highly prized and the greatest of them is Château d'Yquem (*Ee*-calm). While they are sweet wines and usually come at the end of a meal, the French sometimes serve them with the stronger flavored fish such as salmon and smoked fish. (See Chapter 8 on Dessert Wines.)

These five districts produce the great Bordeaux wines, but there are other lesser districts which send floods of ordinary to very good wines to market.

CHATEAU AND REGIONAL BORDEAUX WINES

Bordeaux wines are bottled in four ways.

1. The *proprietary* wines, usually carrying a château name, are the wines grown on one estate, and bottled there. They carry the words "mis en bouteille au château," meaning bottled on the premises. They are expensive wines.

2. The *parish* wines are those grown in a certain town, such as St. Julien or Pauillac, aged and bottled by the shipper. The wines are blends from different vineyards within the legal limits of the parish; they are a step below the haughty château-bottled wines, but may be excellent and fairly costly.

3. *District* bottlings are made of wines grown within the boundaries of Graves or Sauternes or whatever the district may be. They can be very good wines, too, as the shipper may blend for quality. The label will say "Graves" with no town or château name. Such wines should be reasonably priced.

4. Bordeaux Blanc and Bordeaux Rouge are names

This is Château Cheval Blanc, where the famous Claret of that name is produced. The district is St. Émilion, the region Bordeaux.

you'll find on *regional* bottlings. The wine may come from grapes grown anywhere in Bordeaux, blended by the shipper and aged in his cellars. Buy regional bottlings by the reputation of the shipper.

LOOK FOR THE ADEB

The words "appellation controlée" on a bottle of Bordeaux wine assure you that it actually comes from Bordeaux, and the ADEB seal indicates that the wine has been tasted and approved by an impartial jury of Bordeaux shippers who value their reputation. A prominent Bordeaux shipper told me that he had once voted against one of his own wines in a blind tasting of wines for shipment.

"I couldn't believe it," said he. "But I tasted my wine again and found that it was indeed not good enough to ship. So it was *not* shipped."

ADEB stands for "Association pour le Developpement de l'Exportation du Vin de Bordeaux." I think you can understand that, even if you know no French.

NOT ENOUGH WINE

Bordeaux wine shippers are much distressed because they cannot now meet the demand for their fine quality wines. Prices have had to go up because of a succession of poor growing years and also because overpublicizing of a great year like 1959 created a mad scramble for those wines. They quickly sold out, some of them at fantastic prices.

Bordeaux wines of 1961 were even better, and those of 1962 equally good, but the wines of all these years must age to develop their potential greatness. They should last a good thirty years or more, gradually flowering during that time. How many buyers are willing to wait for perfection?

Americans aren't known for patience. Rather than

waiting for a great Bordeaux to develop, it is usually better to settle for less regal wines—parish, district or regional bottlings. They are much cheaper, and can be drunk when you carry them home. The red ones should age well, and the white usually will keep for several years.

In Bordeaux, wine may be compared with a painting or a great work of art. Anyone in Bordeaux can tell you, "Wine is a living thing. It has a birth, it grows to maturity, it ages well or not so well, and finally it dies."

THE WINES OF BURGUNDY

If you follow the road from Dijon to Beaune, you will see most of the vineyards where the great Burgundies originate. This road is only about 35 miles long. The area is a series of hills facing south and east, and some of the most famous vineyards on these hills are only a few acres in size. This is the famous slope of gold, the Côte d'Or.

The upper part of the slope of gold is known as the Côte de Nuits, the lower, the Côtes de Beaune. From the Côte de Nuits come the finest of Burgundies. The most famous of the winegrowing townships or communes are strung along the hills from north to south in this order: Fixin, Gevrey-Chambertin, Morey, Chambolle-Musigny, Vougeot, Flagey-Échezeaux, Vosne-Romanée and Nuits-St. Georges.

Côte de Beaune communes include Aloxe-Corton, Beaune, Pommard, Volnay, Meursault, Puligny-Montrachet and Chassagne-Montrachet.

Do these names sound familiar?

Burgundy names tend to be confusing because the vineyards are broken up into little pieces with individual owners. Take the commune of Gevrey-Chambertin, for example, which incorporates the name of its most famous wine, Le Chambertin. The *grands crus* (great growths, or top quality vineyards) include these separately operated acreages, each entitled to the name Chambertin: Le Chambertin, Chambertin-Clos de Bèze, Chapelle-Chambertin, Charmes-Chambertin, Griotte-Chambertin, Mazis-Chambertin, Mazoyères-Chambertin and Ruchottes-Chambertin.

Next come two dozen *premiers crus*, or first growths, also a part of Gevrey-Chambertin. These would be slightly less expensive wines than the nine grands crus, but they'd be priced higher than the wines labeled simply Gevrey-Chambertin.

Many authorities believe that the greatest wines of Burgundy come from the sixty acres of the commune of Vosne-Romanée. The most majestic name is Romanée Conti whose vineyards are but four and a half acres in size. No wonder the 1959 vintage sold for $15 a bottle! La Romanée wine is produced in two acres of this famous vineyard. Other grand cru names here are Richebourg, Romanée-St. Vivant and La Tâche. If you possess a bottle with any of those labels, you have a treasure.

The wines of the Côte de Beaune are less distinguished and less expensive, because the vineyards are larger and more wine is produced. But they can never be cheap. They are too highly esteemed throughout the world, and there never are enough of them to satisfy the demand. Pommard is the most famous Côte de Beaune wine—Les Épenots a top vineyard.

All of the red Burgundies of the Côte de Nuits and the Côte de Beaune are made of the temperamental pinot noir grape, a delicate, hard-to-grow variety which discourages all but the most ardent winegrowers. It produces deep red, full-bodied wines with a great deal of bouquet. They are often described as "powerful," "virile" and "robust" wines, especially those of the Côte de Nuits. The character of the Burgundy gentles a bit as you go southward. Côte de Beaune wines are "softer," and they mature more quickly. They don't live as long as the great wines, such as Le

THE
WINE REGIONS
OF
UPPER BURGUNDY
(CÔTE D'OR)

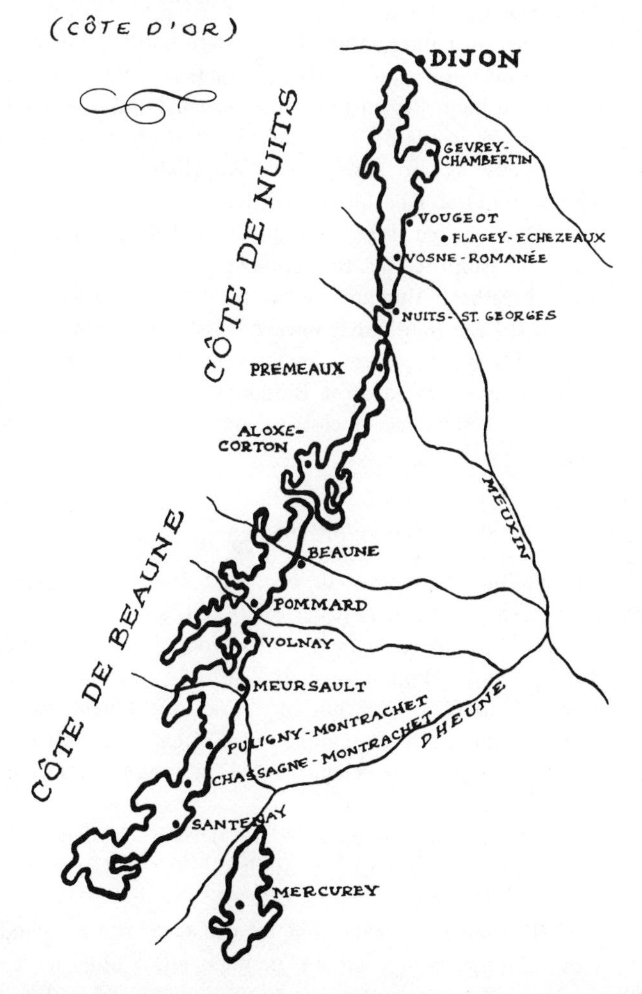

Chambertin and Romanée Conti, which with good care go on mellowing and improving for a good twenty or thirty years.

The dukes of Burgundy claimed to be lords of the finest wines in Christendom, and got no argument about it. They wouldn't today.

The great Burgundies all are estate bottled. There are no châteaus in Burgundy, so the phrase is "mis au Domaine" or "mis en bouteilles au Domaine," usually, and one should look for the words on the label. They are a guarantee of authenticity as are the words "Appellation Controlée," which should also be on the bottle.

Open a red Burgundy an hour before serving it. You'll be surprised at the improvement in taste as the wine "breathes." Burgundy is served at room temperature, and with the most magnificent roasts you can afford. Tournedos Rossini, filet mignon, venison and game birds are fit partners for a great Burgundy at dinner.

The best of recent vintages are 1953, 1955, 1959 and 1961.

THE WHITE WINES OF BURGUNDY

Not all Burgundies are red. There are some famous white ones—Chablis, Pouilly-Fuissé, Meursault and Montrachet. Chablis, the "oyster wine," comes from a legally defined district about 100 miles south and east of Paris, not actually a part of the Côte d'Or, but very close to it. Chablis is the driest of the white Burgundies and often is described as "flinty" in taste. It is delightful with all seafoods and light meats.

The vineyards of Chablis are officially classified. The seven best are Blanchots, Bougros, Clos, Grenouilles, Preuses, Valmur and Vaudésir.

The second classification (the first seven are "grands crus," the next two dozen are "premiers crus," often written "ler cru" on the label) includes the following and no others: Beauroy, Beugnon, Butteaux, Châpelot, Chatain, Côte de Fontenay, Côte de Lechet, Les Forêts, Fourchaume, Les Lys, Melinots, Mont-de-Milieu, Montée de Tonnerre, Montmain, Pied d'Aloup, Sechet, Roncieres, Troeme, Vaillon, Vaucoupin, Vaupinent, Vaulorent, Vosgros, Vogiras.

Look for one of those names plus the name of a grower and the words "mis en bouteille a la propriété" (bottled at the vineyard) or "mise du Domaine" (estate-bottled) when you want a great Chablis.

The Chablis wines of '59 were great, and those of '61, too. Older wines than these are likely to have passed their prime, and in truth many '59's are "over the hill."

Pouilly-Fuissé (*Pwee*-yee-Fwee-*say*) is a dry, heady wine with much bouquet from a little farther south, around Macon. It is a very popular white Burgundy, less aristocratic than the soft, delicate Meursault (*Mere*-so) or the celebrated Montrachet (*Moan*-rah-shay) which Alexander Dumas called divine. All three of these wines are made from the pinot chardonnay grape, as is Chablis. Le Montrachet is considered by many to be the greatest white Burgundy. It costs around $8 a bottle and comes from a vineyard about nineteen acres in size. Two towns, Puligny and Chassagne, have added the name of this great wine to their own. A white wine labeled Puligny-Montrachet or Chassagne-Montrachet is not as fine a wine as one labeled Montrachet. But since the Montrachet vineyards, like most others in Burgundy, are divided among several growers, there should be an owner's name on the label in addition to the name Montrachet: for example, Bouchard Père et Fils.

The soft, delicate Meursault wines should be labeled with the "mise du Domaine" phrase and the name of the vineyard, for example Meursault-Genevrières or Meursault-Charmes.

All white Burgundies are served cold.

THE EXPLOSION OF JOY—BEAUJOLAIS

Lyon, the eating capital of France, is a city situated on three rivers, the Rhône, the Saone—and the Beaujolais. So say the people of Lyon, so fond they are of their red wine. It is a lesser wine than the Burgundies farther north, but it is still considered a Burgundy, even though made of the gamay grape instead of the pinot noir.

Beaujolais, known as "an explosion of joy," is drunk young, the spring after the grapes have been harvested. "It is a light wine; you can drink it all day!" That's what the French say, and they like it especially well with chicken and sausage.

Beaujoláis is drunk cold, not at room temperature as are the greater red wines of Burgundy. It is a fun wine for picnics and back yard barbecues in summer. The best wines of the region are usually labeled Moulin-à-Vent, Morgon, Juliénas, Fleurie or with the name of another township of the region, but the bulk of Beaujolais wines are simply called Beaujolais and nothing more.

CHATEAUNEUF-DU-PAPE, HERMITAGE AND THE WINES OF THE RHONE VALLEY

"Sur le pont d'Avignon," everybody dances. The bridge at Avignon is possibly more celebrated because of the folk song than because it is a remnant of France's early history. But on a wine trail through France, one learns that Avignon, the capital of Christendom in the fourteenth century, is the southern boundary of France's Côtes du Rhône wine district.

The Côtes du Rhône region is below Burgundy, and west and north of Côtes de Provence from whence our country has been getting some lovely Rosé wines in the

Wines aging in the cask in cellars of the Côtes du Rhône district of France. Châteauneuf-du-Pape and Hermitage are famous wines from this region.

last several years. Two even more famous Rosés come from Côtes du Rhône, very near Avignon. They are Tavel (Tah-*vell*) and Lirac (*Lee*-rock) pink wines, and they are very choice. But the most interesting wines from the Rhône Valley are Châteauneuf-du-Pape and Hermitage.

The Côtes du Rhône region extends from Avignon to Lyon. It is about 125 miles long and is broken in the middle by a gap of forty miles where no grapes are grown. South of the vineless area, grapes still are warmed by the Mediterranean sun. From sun-warmed slopes come the wines of Châteauneuf-du-Pape. At the other end of the region, northward, the climate is colder, the hills are steep and the wines have an entirely different character. Hermitage wines are grown in the northern Rhône valley near Valence.

It is incredible in what poor soils grapes thrive. The vineyards of Châteauneuf-du-Pape ("new palace of the Pope," named for the summer home of one of the seven French popes of the middle ages, ruins of which are a landmark) are thickly pebbled. During the heat of the day the stones inhale the sun's warmth and at night they give it back to the vines. Here the *mistral*, an ill wind that blows *nobody* good, rages for weeks at a time, and vineyards must be protected by windbreaks—more toil for the hard-working grower.

Châteauneuf-du-Pape is a full-bodied, fruity red wine, resembling a Burgundy. It is rare for a red table wine to have such quality from a warm area and low elevation. Alcohol content is 12½ per cent or more, and the wine is highly regarded as a partner for roasts, especially beef, and game. It is one of the best of cheese wines. Like Burgundy, it needs to "breathe" in the opened bottle for an hour before it is served. Cool room temperature does it justice.

GASPARD THE HERMIT

At the upper end of the vineless area of the Rhône valley, the equally famous, distinguished red and white wines of Hermitage are grown on steep, terraced hillsides. There is a romantic story to celebrate them.

In the days when knights were bold and battled for the favors of fair ladies, along about the year 1225, Gaspard de Stiremberg, courtier of Queen Blanche of Castile, grew tired of tourneys and knight errantry and decided to become a hermit. He galloped off into the Rhône Valley, took a fancy to these steep hills and built a hermitage on the top of one of the highest of them. He had brought along syrah grape cuttings, acquired on a crusade to the Holy Land, for although Gaspard could do without people, he could not be a proper hermit without wine. His wines flourished and their descendants produce the grapes for the Hermitage wines produced in the area of Tain L'Hermitage, the village named for Gaspard the Hermit.

North of Tain another famous Rhône valley wine is produced. It is Côte Rôtie (Wrote-*ee*), red, full-bodied, long-lived and highly esteemed. Close by is the district of Condrieu, famous for its white wine, Château Grillet (Gree-*yay*).

Hermitage red wines are in the cask for six years and may live for twenty. They are served with magnificent roasts, game, red meats and cheese. Hermitage white wines are distinguished, too, and are served most frequently with fish, seafoods and light meats. Côte Rôtie and Condrieu wines are served with the same food groups, the red with meats, the Château Grillet of Condrieu with fish.

The red wines, at cool room temperature, are opened an hour early; the whites are served chilled, but not so cold as to restrain their fragrances.

WINES OF THE VALLEY OF THE LOIRE

The wines of the Loire are grown in a direct line with those of Burgundy, but the grapes are the grapes of Bordeaux. Most Loire wines are white ones, light in alcohol and flowery. Vouvray, the most famous wine of this region, is sweet, naturally sparkling and has more alcohol in it. Some of the best Vouvrays mature over a period of years, and may keep twenty or thirty years or more. But most wines of the Loire are short-lived and meant to be drunk young and fresh.

The region is famous for its châteaus as well as its wines. Tourists who travel this route are likely to meet with wines they cannot obtain in this country, much to their later disappointment.

Anjou produces a famous Rosé wine as well as white. Muscadet, Reuilly, Quincy, Sancerre and Pouilly are other town and wine names in the valley of the Loire. From Pouilly comes Pouilly-Fumé which is often confused with its Burgundy neighbor, Pouilly-Fuissé. It is made from the sauvignon grape, not the chardonnay of Burgundy. It was Marie Antoinette's favorite wine.

Chinon and Bourgueil produce red wines, the former said to have the smell of violets, the latter the taste of raspberries.

Loire wines usually are drunk well-chilled, with fish dishes and light luncheon foods.

THE BRANDY KNOWN AS COGNAC

Most winemaking regions of the world distill some of their wines to make brandy, or use the leavings of winemaking for the purpose. Nowhere but in France does brandy-

Many of the women who pick grapes for the wine which produces cognac, in the Charente region of France, still wear the wide-brimmed sun-bonnets known as "quichenotte" (keesh-not). They were dubbed "kiss-nots" by sailors, which the girls translated into a French-sounding equivalent.

making reach such perfection. Brandy in France is known as "eau de vie," or water of life.

It is not just brandy, but a distillate of wines made from grapes grown in the Charente region of France, just above Bordeaux, where the climate and soil, plus time-tested distilling methods and years of aging in oak casks, produce a rare and fiery liquid. It takes forty to fifty years to produce a great brandy, eight to ten years to make a good one.

The Cognac region is divided into seven zones or "crus," each producing a distinctive brandy. In order of the quality of brandy, they are known as Grande Champagne, Petite Champagne, Borderies, Fins-Bois, Bons-Bois, Bois-Ordinaires and Bois-Communs. Cognacs are produced in several qualities, depending upon the blends of brandies used from the various districts. "Fine Champagne" cognac is one made of at least 50 per cent Grande Champagne brandy, the rest Petite Champagne.

VSOP on the label of a cognac bottle means "very superior old pale"; VO means "very old"; OC is "old cognac"; VVG is "very very good" and Three-Star is a symbol used to indicate a good blend consistent on its own level.

Cognac is a favorite after-dinner liqueur but also is served "on the rocks" or as a highball with soda or water, before a meal. It is the gourmet's choice for flaming food.

6. GERMAN, ITALIAN AND SWISS WINES

Wine rejoices the heart of man, and joy is the Mother of all virtue.—Johann Wolfgang von Goethe

THE RHINE WINES AND MOSELLES OF GERMANY

Germany's Rhine and Moselle wines rank with France's Bordeaux and Burgundies as the world's Grade A-plus, four-star, extra-special, gourmet's choice white wines.* Light and delicate, fragrant and flowery, they are all wines ranging in alcoholic content from 8 to 11 per cent. They aren't wines to forget in a cellar; they are best when not over five or six years old. The 1959 Rhine wines and Moselles were among the finest, but they are growing old.

* Germany grows some red wines, but they are not outstanding and are consumed at home.

Rhine wines come in brown bottles, Moselles in green. The choice Rhine wines and all of the Moselles are made from the noble riesling grape, which makes good wines in other parts of the world, including California, but saves its best efforts for its homeland, the slopes bordering the Rhine and its tributaries. The Moselles are the northernmost vineyards of Europe. It is rather remarkable that vines should flourish in the latitude of Labrador, but the riesling can take chilly weather, rocky soil and steep hillsides—the southern slopes that catch the sun. And with constant care and toil on the part of the vintner, this small green grape ripens to yield juices for some of the greatest wines in the world. In exceptional years, when frost is late and *edelfäule* ("noble rot") has done its work, rare *beerenauslese* and *trockenbeerenauslese* wines may be produced (see pages 128 to 132). These sweet wines do age well. They are more liqueur than table wine, however.

THOSE NAMES ON THE BOTTLES

Labels on German wines are very confusing to one who does not understand that every word is there for a purpose and tells a story.

There's the date: that's understandable. And the district: Rheingau, Rheinhessen, Rheinpfalz, Moselle or another. Then, on the best wines, there's the name of the town, plus the name of the vineyard. The town name has "er" added to it—the wine is a "Forster" if it comes from Forst, a "Deidesheimer" if it comes from Deidesheim. Thus we may have a wine called Forster Kirchenstuck, Niersteiner Oelberg or Wehlener Sonnenuhr, the second name being that of the vineyard.

Other words you should understand when you find them on a label are these:

Original-Abfüllung: Bottled by the grower. It corresponds to the "mise en bouteille au domaine" of Burgundy. If the wine comes from one of the bigger estates which has a castle, the words *schlossabfüllung* or *schlossabzug* may be used to indicate the wine was bottled at the castle. All of the finest German wines will be labeled by one or another of these names.

A typical label from a bottle of German wine, illustrating the various terms explained in this chapter.

Spätlese: Late picking. The wine was made from grapes picked after the normal harvest, in good years. In 1962, some grapes were picked as late as Christmas! Spätlese on a label is an indication of quality better than average. The wine is full, fragrant, on the sweet side.

Auslese: "Selection." This word indicates a wine made from selected bunches of grapes. It is a high quality wine, and usually expensive. *Beerenauslese* indicates "berry selection" or a picking of individual grapes, and *trockenbeerenauslese* is the "dry berry selection," which doesn't sound as enticing as it is. The latter two wines are rich, sweet, liqueur-like beverages which can be made only in exceptional years. They are expensive, especially *trockenbeerenauslese.*

Naturrein or *naturwein:* A natural wine without any sugar added. In poor years it may be necessary to add sugar to aid in fermentation.

Cabinet or *kabinett:* Originally a private reserve of the vineyard owner. Rather meaningless now.

Eis-wein: 1961 and 1962 were rare years in which sharp, freezing rains came to German vineyards, permitting vintners to make winc from frozen ripe grapes. Eis-wein is luscious, and expensive.

THE THREE IMPORTANT RHINE DISTRICTS

Rheingau, Rheinhessen and Rheinpfalz (Palatinate) are the three names to remember. Note them on the map, page 97.

THE RHEINGAU

The Rhine river makes a sharp westward bend above Mainz in its northerly course from the Swiss border. In this bend, on the right bank from Mainz to Bingen and Rudesheim, grow the greatest wines of Germany in an area only twenty miles long. The vines look south, catching the sun; they are protected by mountains in the rear; and the Rhine, wide and deep in this bend, tempers the weather. Famous names in this area of only 6,575 acres include Johannisberg (and Schloss Johannisberg),* Schloss Vollrads, Hattenheim, Hallgarten, Steinberg, Erbach and of course Rudesheim and Hochheim, from which the British get their term "hock" which they apply to Rhine wines.

* A wine so famous it is known as Castle (Schloss) Johannisberg instead of as "Johannisberger" with a following vineyard name.

Rheingau wines don't need to be labeled "Riesling." You may assume that they are made from riesling grapes.

THE RHEINHESSEN

Below the Rheingau, from Bingen to Worms on the left bank of the Rhine, lie the vineyards of the Rheinhessen with an acreage six times greater than that of the Rheingau. The wines produced in these 150 or more villages are not as famous as those of the Rheingau, but they are many and their volume is large. They are fruity, fragrant, soft and ingratiating, very popular with Americans. The bottle tells you if the riesling grape is in it. Otherwise you can assume the sylvaner, a less aristocratic grape but a more productive one, or a mixture of several varieties, was used.

From this area comes *Liebfraumilch* (literally "milk of the blessed mother"). Worms was the home of the original Liebfraumilch, but now it is made in most villages of the Rheinhessen. It is not a wine of any standing. Liebfraumilch is a blended wine, and may be good, bad or indifferent. The name of the shipper is its character reference. Good labels include Blue Nun, Hans Christoff, Madonna and Glockenspiel.

Bodenheim, Nackenheim, Nierstein, Laubenheim, Oppenheim (many of the towns in this district have names ending in "heim" or home) are some of the familiar Rheinhessen names. Bingen and Worms are others.

Look for the vineyard name on the best wines from the Rheinhessen (Binger Scharlachberg, Niersteiner Heiligenbaum, for example) and for "Original Abfüllung."

THE RHEINPFALZ OR PALATINATE

This area, below the Rheinhessen, was famous in Roman times for its plentitude of wines. The acreage is about seven times that of the Rheingau. Most Rheinpfalz wines are everyday wines, but some are distinguished. Town names include Wachenheim, Deidesheim, Forst and Ruppertsberg. The Rheinpfalz borders on France; some of its wines are like Alsatian wines.

Only 10 per cent of the wines from the Rheinpfalz are made from the riesling; most use the sylvaner, muller-thurgau and the traminer grape which produces a spicy wine. When the riesling is used, the label says so. Because these vineyards are farther south, they may do well in years of poor vintage in the Rheingau or Rheinhessen, and in good years most of the *beerenauslese* and *trockenbeerenauslese* wines produced come from this area.

TWO MINOR WINE DISTRICTS

The Nahe valley is one of the lesser districts of the Rhine. The Nahe river flows into the Rhine at Bingen, and the Nahe vineyards produce wines of varied character because of differences in soil. Some of them are of top quality.

The region of Franconia centers in Wurzburg and produces "harder" wines than the other areas. They come in a squatty flask known as *bocksbeutel.*

THE MOSELLES

Moselle (Mosel) wines come from vineyards on the steep banks of the Moselle, which joins the Rhine at Coblenz, north of the Rheingau, and from its tributaries, the Ruwer and the Saar. Moselle wines are always labeled "Mosel-Saar-Ruwer"; they are always made from riesling grapes, and in addition to being very light, fresh and flowery, they often are slightly *spritzig,* or naturally sparkling. Many wine-lovers become poetic over Moselle wines.

Strict laws govern the vintage along the Moselle as along the Rhine. Local boards of citizens meet to determine the date for the vintage to begin, and church bells ring

THE WINE REGIONS OF GERMANY

COBLENZ
WINNINGEN
MOSELLE RIVER
OBER-WESEL
RHEINGAU
LORCH
WIESBADEN
RUDESHEIM
ASSMANNSHAUSEN
HOCHHEIM
INGELHEIM
BINGEN
MAINZ
LAUBENHEIM
NAHE
BODENHEIM
KREUZNACH
NACKENHEIM
NIERSTEIN
OPPENHEIM
RHINE RIVER
RHEINHESSEN
WORMS
LIEBFRAUMILCH
KALLSTADT
MANNHEIM
DURKHEIM
RHEINPFALZ
(PALATINATE)
WACHENHEIM
FORST
DEIDESHEIM
RUPPERTSBERG
SPEYER

as a signal for the picking of the ripe grapes. Festivities accompany the beginning of the harvest in most villages. These are great fun for tourists who happen along.

The better known Moselles are expensive (often $6 or $7 a bottle). Some of the village names are Bernkastel, Trittenheim, Graach, Piesport, Wehlen, Zeltingen. The best wines from these towns will also carry a vineyard name (Bernkasteler Doktor, Piesporter Goldtropfchen, Zeltingen Schlossberg, for example), plus the words *original abfüllung.* The less good wines may be called simply Bernkasteler Riesling, Piesporter, etc. These are blended, sometimes sugared wines bottled by a shipper.* They cannot, of course, be labeled *original-abfüllung* or *naturrein.*

Moselblumchen, like the Liebfraumilch of the Rheinhessen, is ordinary blended wine.

Moselles are so light they should be drunk before they are four years old, with the exception of a few great wines.

HOW TO SERVE GERMAN WINES

Many wine-lovers prefer German wines for drinking alone, without food, because of their delicacy. Some of these wines are so light that in California they couldn't be legally classed as wines.

Serve Rhines and Moselles cold, but not too cold, and when you serve them with food or at a meal, make sure the food flavors are not rich or spicy or sharp. Rhine wines are good with roast chicken, turkey or veal, and with the bland-flavored fishes. Moselles often are served with filet of sole, Dover sole, trout or oysters.

Rhine wines are frequently mixed with sparkling water to make "wine and seltzer," a tall cold drink for summer. They are excellent in wedding punches (see pages 150 to

* In a poor year, wine with sugar added may be better than natural wine. Sugared wine is not necessarily sweeter on the tongue, as the sugar must be fermented into alcohol.

155). The expensive aristocrats among them shouldn't be diluted. Keep them for special occasions. If they're to appear on the dinner table, we might well be advised by a couplet from Eugene Field:

> "When I demanded of my friend what viands he preferred,
> He quoth: 'A large cold bottle and a small hot bird.' "

Or a small hot fish?

THE TABLE WINES OF ITALY

CHIANTI ISN'T THE ONLY ITALIAN RED WINE

Chianti, the wine of Tuscany, is Italian wine in the minds of most Americans. But Chianti, in its familiar raffia-wrapped flask, known as a *fiasco* (plural, *fiaschi*), is but one of hundreds of wines from a country that is a vast vineyard producing over a billion gallons of wine a year. In Italy everybody drinks wine, and almost everybody grows grapes in his own back yard. Next to France, Italy produces most of the world's wines.

When you travel throughout Italy ask for the wines of the region, and you'll have some delightful experiences. Many of this country's most pleasing wines are poor travelers and never reach our shores, but more than 700 varieties do, and imports from Italy increased more than 20 per cent in 1962.

Italian winegrowers are beginning to take pains with some of their wines which many authorities believe could match the Clarets of France if given sufficient care. Great rivers of mass-produced Italian wines are exported, but there are some ruby jewels.

The country's best of all wines come from the north,

especially the Piedmont region, where vines are grown as in France, on the ground. Elsewhere they are draped upon trees, walls and fences, picturesquely but in haphazard fashion.

Italy's pride, the "wine of kings" is *Barolo*, from a strictly defined area around the village of Barolo, south of Turin (Torino), in the Piedmont. Barolo, made from the aristocratic nebbiolo grape, is a deep ruby wine which has been described variously as "velvety," "generous, yet austere," "having the perfume of violets" and "definitely a great wine." It has been compared to Hermitage or Côte Rotie of France's Rhône valley.

Barolo is aged in wood for about three years, then is bottled in the Burgundy bottle, after which it usually is aged further before it is drunk. Barolo will keep for over fifteen years. Its traditional table companions are venison and magnificent roasts; it is not an everyday wine, and unfortunately, not too much is available. *Gattinara*, equally distinguished, and from the same grape and same region, smells of violets, tastes of raspberries and ages well.

Barbaresco is Barolo's younger brother. From the same grapes, "the poor man's Barolo" is grown around the outer boundaries of the Barolo district. It is a lighter, softer wine, which may be aged, but usually is drunk younger than Barolo.

There are so many B wines in the alphabet of Italy's viniculture that it is easy to become confused. *Bardolino*, from vines grown on the eastern shore of Italy's largest lake, Lake Garda, in the north, is an excellent light red wine, usually drunk from one to three years old. Bardolino is the wine of Verona, where Romeo wooed Juliet and where the Etruscans and the Romans grew vines and made famous wines. Neighboring red wines are the famous *Valpolicella* and *Valpantena*, full-bodied, dry and charming wines to accompany red meats to the table.

Other good red table wines of the north include

Grignolino, the best of which is remindful of Barolo, though it is lighter-bodied, and *Freisa,* a fruity, mellow wine with a taste reminding one of raspberries.

Now comes another B wine: *Barbera,* named for its grape, a rough, full-bodied wine, slightly sweet, to serve, like Chianti, with strongly seasoned foods. In Italy the trouble with naming a wine for its grape is that in another part of the country the same grape may yield an entirely different wine because of differences in soil and climate. California makes a Barbera from this grape—and it is a very different wine from the Italian.

CHIANTI, AND CHIANTI CLASSICO

Most Chiantis are sold when they are about six months old. They are rough and ready wines for spaghetti suppers, picnics and informal meals featuring highly seasoned foods. These are the wines that usually come in the straw covered fiaschi. Oddly, this typical "peasant" bottle has now become more expensive than the ordinary wine bottle because of its handmade wrappings. For this reason we may be seeing the cheaper wines from Italy in the Claret type bottles which are used for aged wines. Some of the better wines are now bottled in the picturesque fiaschi. You can't judge the quality of a wine by its container any more!

Chianti Classico is quality *Chianti*, which must come (since 1932) from the hills of a strictly defined district between Florence and Siena. Some Chiantis Classico are aged moderately; others are meant to be consumed young. They are velvety, ruby- or garnet-colored wines, decidedly masculine and meant for meats and game. They are made in a centuries-old manner, from a blend of grapes, primarily the sangiovese (sahn-gee-oh-*veh*-seh).

Brolio Chianti (another B!) from the vineyards of Baron Ricasoli, is a famous one. Grapes for it are cultivated as they are in Piedmont, an exception for the Tuscany region.

Lambrusco is an interesting red wine produced in the vicinity of Bologna, home of Italy's richest menu and most famous sausages. Lambrusco is naturally *frizzante*,* that is, it has a natural sparkle which subsides soon after pouring.

* In French, *pétillant;* in German, *spritzig.*

Lambrusco and another red of the region, *Sangiovese* (from that grape), are particularly suited to the *grasso* (fat) foods of Bologna.

Falerno, a wine praised by Horace, is a red (sometimes white) wine from near Rome which some modern critics think does not live up to its 2,000-year-old reputation. It was "divine" or "immortal" Falernian wine then; perhaps we expect too much of it.

South of Tuscany the red table wines are not noteworthy, but there are many excellent sweet wines from southern Italy.

THE TEARS OF CHRIST AND OTHER WHITE TABLE WINES

Most famous of Italy's white table wines is *Asti Spumante,* discussed in Chapter 8.

There are white Chiantis to go with fish instead of meat. *Lugana,* "the fish wine" from the shores of Lake Garda, comes in a tall, slim, green, three-sided bottle with a fish-shaped tag around its neck. *Termeno* (traminer), from near Venice, is a deep straw color, rich and yet dry. *Verdicchio* (Ver-*deek*-yoh) is a mellow white wine much liked in this country; *Orvieto* (Or-vee-*et*-oh), from Umbria, once the favorite of popes, is called "a ladies' wine" by many Italians. (They *need* a ladies' wine in Italy!) Orvieto is frequently shipped in a fiasco. Then there's *Frascati,* much favored in Rome, and like the others, good to drink while eating fish, though not considered anything very special.

Lacrima Christi (tear of Christ), is a golden, semi-dry wine grown on the slopes of Mount Vesuvius. Like other wines grown in volcanic soil, it possesses a distinctive bouquet. Legend tells us that the wine was named in this way:

Lucifer, hurled from heaven, fell into what is now the Bay of Naples, carrying along a portion of paradise. Christ, looking down and seeing that human wickedness existed even on this bit of heaven, shed a tear of divine pity, which fell upon a vine. That vine flourished and ever since has yielded a marvelous wine, the "tears of Christ."

Some Lacrima Christi is shipped to the north where it is subjected to a secondary fermentation in the bottle, becoming a somewhat sweet sparkling wine. There is also a red Lacrima Christi which is a good wine when aged.

A very popular white Italian wine is *Soave* (So-*ah*-veh), from near Verona in the north. Soave, as its name implies, is soft, smooth and dry, a perfect partner for fish, seafood, eggs and chicken.

One of the driest whites of Italy is the delicate, fragrant *Capri,* best when it comes from the isle and not from the mainland where it has imitators. *Vernaccia* (Ver-*nah*-chee-ah) is a bright amber wine, very dry but strong, mellow and velvety. Strangely enough it is considered a dessert wine as well as a companion for fish.

There is an interesting story about a white wine from Montefiascone, one much like Orvieto, which is called *Est! Est!! Est!!!* with a varying number of exclamation marks. It comes both dry and sweet.

Once upon a time, the story goes, a wine-loving German bishop was summoned to Rome. As was the custom of the day, he sent a servant ahead to mark the way and to find the best accommodations. The servant was asked particularly to check the wines along the road to Rome. If a tavern served good wine, the servant was to mark upon the shutters the word *est.* (If you remember your first lesson in Latin, you'll know that *est* means *it is.*) Occasionally, when the wine was exceptional, the servant wrote *est-est!* But when the man tasted the wine of Montefiascone, a hundred miles short of Rome, he scrawled in huge letters on the shutters, *Est! Est!! Est!!!*

The good bishop, following along later, agreed with that judgment, never got to Rome and, I regret to report, is said to have drunk himself to death on that beautiful wine. His tomb bears the inscription:

Propter nimium Est Est Est
Dominus noster mortuus est.

("On account of too much *Est Est Est* our master is dead.")

THE ROSÉ WINES OF ITALY

Rosés have been produced widely in Italy only for the last twenty years. None can match the best of French and American, but there are some pleasing ones including *Chiaretto del Garda* (from Lake Garda, of course, a good recommendation in itself); *Collameno Rosé, Orvieto Rosé, Rosatello, Rosé Antinori* and *Vinrosa.* Several of these are brand names.

Vermouths, made all over Italy, are discussed in Chapter 9, and the country's most famous dessert wine, Marsala, on page 124.

ITALIAN WINES AND FOOD

Italians serve their full-bodied red wines with all kinds of game, beefsteaks, rich stews, curries, roast turkey, duck or goose and roast meats, also with all kinds of sausages and the spicy cheeses such as gorgonzola, parmesan and sharp cheddar.

Their lighter red wines and robust Rosés, both dry and semi-sweet, are served with roast and fried chicken, poultry or meat pies, breaded veal cutlets, lamb chops, beef tongue, veal or lamb loaf and croquettes of these meats. They're served with highly flavored fish and seafood dishes, smoked fish, rich tomato-sauced dishes and all the wonderful spaghetti, macaroni and rice dishes for which Italy is famed. These wines are served with pizzas, too, and with antipasto and all kinds of cheese.

The dry white wines of Italy, and the light Rosés, are served with bland and delicate dishes such as subtly flavored fish and seafoods, cream soups, simple pastas prepared with fish or seafood, cheese dishes made with the blander cheeses (cream, cottage, ricotta, mozzarella). Soufflés, egg dishes, pork prepared in a simple manner and chicken a la king are other partners for dry white wines.

The semi-sweet white wines and light Rosés also are served with stronger-flavored foods such as bouillabaisse, lobster thermidor, fried oysters and scallops, creamed vegetables, baked or candied sweet potatoes, Virginia ham and cheeses of all kinds, excepting usually the strongest ones for which robust red wines are preferred.

At wine-tastings of Italian red and white wines and Vermouths, the accompanying foods usually include platters of cheese: cubes of fontina, parmesan and bel paese (this cheese is soft and it usually is better to serve it whole, with a knife, for soft cubes are hard to spear on a pick). Paper-thin slices of Italian sausages such as salami, peperoni and coppa (cured pork shoulder) may appear. If you can get packaged delicacies such as small, poppy-seeded bread sticks (grissini) and thumbnail-sized almond macaroons (amarettini), these are pleasant to munch while sipping Italian wines.

It should be noted that a red government seal, the *marchio nazionale,* is attached to the necks of bottles of Italian wines from delimited areas, guaranteeing that the *Chianti Classico,* for example, is from the ancient Chianti district, or that the Valpolicella is from Verona.

THE WINES OF SWITZERLAND

There's plenty of evidence to show that winegrowing has been going on in Switzerland for 2,000 years, but until recently the Swiss have been drinking most of their wines themselves. Now Americans have acquired a taste for them; our imports have more than doubled since 1960. The ever-toiling Swiss are now carving out new vineyards on slopes sometimes so steep that no machine can be brought to lighten the labor.

What we like about Swiss wines is their light, dry, friendly character. Most Swiss wines are white. Those grown in the German-speaking part of Switzerland resemble Rhine wines; those grown near Italy have some of the characteristics of Italian wines; and those grown in the French-speaking region known as La Suisse Romande are Switzerland's best wines. The cantons of Neuchatel, Vaud and Valais in French-speaking Switzerland produce nearly three-fourths of the wines.

Many of these wines are *pétillant*, or slightly sparkling, especially the ingratiating Neuchatel, which is called "the starry wine." Pour it from a height of between 12 and 18 inches, lifting the bottle and lowering it as the wine streams into your glass, and you will find a star. The bubbles foam on the surface, then gradually subside, leaving a fallen star in your glass!

The Swiss Romande possesses some of the country's most spectacular scenery—blue lakes, steep mountain slopes and old castles including Chillon, made famous by Lord Byron. The castle of Chillon is in the canton of Vaud bordering the northern shores of Lake Leman, or Lake Geneva as it is familiarly known.

The lake shore town of Vevey since before the seventeenth century has celebrated a "Fete des Vignerons" every twenty-five years. If you'd like to see this fabulous national celebration honoring wines and winegrowers, mark your calendar for 1980. The last fete was held in 1955.

Vaud's toiling vineyardists take their work seriously and while they respect authority, they can be critical. The story is told of a Vaudois peasant who, surveying his ruined vines after a hailstorm, shook his fist at the heavens and exclaimed, "I won't name Anyone, *but this is disgusting!*"

Major producer of Swiss wines, Vaud divides its vintages at Lausanne into two main groups, Lavaux, from east of the city, and La Cote, from west, both districts bordering the lake of Geneva. Lavaux is picturesque with its steeply terraced hillsides rising sharply from the lake, almost defying gravity.

Vaud's wines include, from Lavaux, *Dezaley, Epesses, Rivaz, St. Saphorin;* and from La Cote, a wine of that name and *Fechy, Luins, Begnins. Yvorne* and *Aigle* are white wines of a "racier" quality, grown along the Rhône valley just below the lake. Most of these wines are named for their villages.

The third important winegrowing canton is Valais, the "vieux pays," or old country, which borders Italy on the south and France on the west. The Rhône has its source here, and sheltered by the high rising Alps, Valais basks in warmth and sun. Tradition is observed here when the people of Anniviers come down from their mountain village homes with marching songs, fifes and drums to begin their work in the vineyards. In October, after the harvest, they carry eight-gallon barrels of new wine back to their villages where they leave it to mature in larchwood casks for ten to fifteen years.

Here in Valais the vineyards are very steep and water is scarce. By long, continuous toil the winegrowers have carved winding aqueducts around the mountains—miles

Vineyards in Switzerland provide breath-taking backdrops. This grape-growing region in the canton of Vaud lies along the Rhône Valley just below Lake Geneva and produces the "racy" white wine known as Aigle, named for its village.

and miles of them. In winter the vineyard tenders do not rest, for they must carry back up the mountains all the soil washed into the valleys by rains. No wonder the Swiss prize their hard-won wines!

Valais wines include *Fendant*, probably the most popular of all Swiss wines, *Dole*, one of the few reds (which is served chilled, like the whites—it is made from burgundy grapes), *Johannisberg* similar to Rhine wine, with full-bodied flavor that has won it the appellation "prince of love," and a sweet dessert wine known as *Malvorsie*.

From the Italian-speaking region, Ticino, come smooth, fruity red wines such as *Merlot*, *Nostrano*, *Nebbiolo*, *Bondola*. Merlot is the one you are most likely to find, I believe.

There is a lovely Rosé known as *Oeil de Perdrix* (partridge's eye) from Neuchatel, and other pink Swiss wines are beginning to be known in this country.

Most books on wine give very little space to Swiss wines, probably because so few have been available to us until now. The situation is changing rapidly largely because of our lust for travel abroad and the immediate appeal which Swiss wines have for the American palate. Swiss wines usually are inexpensive, and there's another enticement.

All Swiss wines are served chilled, even the red Dole. Neuchatel and Dezaley are served throughout the meal. Neuchatel goes into, and accompanies the famous fondue. All of the wines are "cheese" wines (what else would you expect in Switzerland?), and all of the whites are suitable for serving with all cheese, fish and chicken dishes. The reds usually accompany beef and game.

Swiss wines sometimes are called "luncheon" wines, because they are such good companions for luncheon foods. But they are pleasing any time of day. For a Swiss wine-tasting, one would serve Swiss and gruyere cheeses.

THE CARNOTSET IN SWITZERLAND

Almost all Swiss wine cellars have their carnotsets, or wine-tasting rooms. Some of these date from ancient times, and are elaborately decorated with symbols of the vine and wine-growing.

A fourteenth-century mural in a Swiss carnotset tells a Greek legend in these words:

> When men began to drink
> They burst into song, like birds.
> When they drank more
> They became strong as lions,
> When they drank too much
> They became stupid as asses.

The Swiss attribute their good health and longevity to their wines. Who knows but that they're right!

7. THE "GENEROUS" WINES: SHERRY, PORT AND MADEIRA

A table without wine is like a stew without meat.
–Spanish proverb

SHERRY IS FOR JEREZ

Spain's great gift to the world is Sherry, a blended wine fortified with brandy to raise its alcoholic content to around 20 per cent. Sherry is so universally savored, especially as an appetizer wine, that it is imitated in almost every wine-growing country. But true Sherry comes only from the vicinity of Jerez de la Frontera, Spain. It is made from palomino grapes grown in chalky soil, it is sun-baked in the cask, then blended by a unique process known as the "solera system."

In the spacious bodegas (storage houses) of Jerez de la Frontera, Sherry casks are stacked in three tiers, establishing a solera. When wine is shipped, once or twice a year, up to 30 per cent of a bottom cask may be drawn off. It is replaced from the second tier, and that amount is replaced from the top cask of the stack, which in turn is filled by wine which has aged for several years in the hot sun in preparation for this blending. The process goes on decade after decade, century after century. Sherries are always being blended. There are no vintage years for Sherry; Sherry is a complexity of wines from many different years.

Many of the casks in which Sherry matures and is blended are made of American white oak. They ride the Atlantic full of wine on the way over, and after the Sherry is bottled on our shores, the barrels are taken apart, stave by stave, for the return trip, in order to take up less room. The dismantling necessitates a great deal of labor in the bodegas, for they are tricky to reassemble. Used Sherry casks are in great demand for aging whiskey.

In the bodegas of Gonzalez-Byass in Jerez, which I have visited, stand giant casks bearing the crests of the royal houses of Europe. These casks are kept full even though the kings and queens whose names they bear may be long dead. Unique are century-old casks with hand carving representing Christ and the twelve apostles. The "Christo" holds 3,500 gallons of Sherry; it is the largest wine cask in the world.

In one special bodega a huge cask of Sherry is dedicated to Winston Churchill in honor of his eightieth birthday. Other casks of ordinary size (one of them is Generalissimo Francisco Franco's) are autographed by famous persons. Tourists may visit these bodegas which produce five Spanish brandies as well as thirty-two Sherries, of which the light appetizer Sherry known as Tio Pepe ("Uncle Joe") is the most popular.

HOW SHERRY GOT ITS NAME

The British penchant for mangling difficult words is responsible for the name "Sherry." Unable to pronounce Jerez, a name to stop most Americans, too, they first called this highly prized wine "Jerz," then "Jerries," and finally slipped into the easier "Sherry." Sherry is Xérès to the Frenchman, and the French cook has found several special uses for his neighbor's wine.

THE KINDS OF SPANISH SHERRY

Spain's great wine comes dry or sweet, with many gradations between. In general, Sherries are classed as *fino* (dry) or *oloroso* (sweet).

Manzanilla is the driest of all Spanish Sherries; some say it is the driest wine in the world. It is an appetizer Sherry with a salt tang and isn't well-known outside of Spain.

Fino, or dry Sherry, is the popular cocktail type to serve before dinner. Americans have developed quite a passion for Spain's fino Sherries.

Amontillado (remember Edgar Allen Poe's shivery "Cask of Amontillado"?) is an in-between, neither dry nor sweet, and just great for serving to guests who drop in at any old time. This is a general purpose Sherry, a good one to have always on hand.

Oloroso Sherries are the sweet ones from Spain, the equivalent of our "cream" or "golden" types. They are rich and deep amber in color (funny thing, even this dark Sherry is classed as a "white" wine!). Oloroso means fragrant, and olorosos are. They are dessert or after-dessert wines, good with fruit or cakes or pastry, or cheese or nuts. You may find oloroso Sherries sub-classified as *amoroso, cream* or *brown* Sherry, named in order of color depth and sweetness. Brown

Sherry is deeply colored, and just about as rich and sweet as a perceptive palate can enjoy it.

THE KINDS OF AMERICAN SHERRY

Both California and New York produce Sherries, but they aren't quite the same. Most of them are scientifically heat-treated for quick maturing. They are much less expensive than Spanish Sherries, and more people can afford them.

California can grow palomino grapes and has the sun for Spain's method of producing Sherry, so some serious-minded vintners have established soleras and even import Spanish "flor," the film yeast which grows in fino wines and which is responsible for much of the flavor and bouquet. Several eastern Sherries are produced by a modified solera system.

In general our Sherries can be classed as follows:

Pale Dry is a "bone-dry" appetizer wine to serve chilled before dinner.

Cocktail Sherry, a dry appetizer wine, is a growing favorite to serve chilled, "on the rocks," or in mixed drinks. As the name suggests, it is a party beverage of distinction.

Sherry, without qualifications, is an in-between, neither dry nor sweet, and generally pleases most appetites. It is a good safe choice to offer guests whose preferences aren't known.

Cream or *Golden Sherry* is deep amber and sweet. This is the dessert wine, the accompaniment for cheese, fruit, fruit cake, pastry.

Select Sherries are those aged in the Spanish way, usually made from palomino grapes. They may compare well with Spanish Sherries, and while more expensive than other American Sherries, are less costly than Spain's.

HOW TO KEEP AND STORE SHERRY

This most accommodating wine can take a lot of abuse. It does not improve in the bottle so there's no reason for storing it away in a wine cellar. Keep it handy in the refrigerator, if there's room. Or keep it on the pantry shelf. Even an opened bottle of the sweeter Sherries will keep for weeks or even months in a cupboard, if you'll let it. The dry Sherries, the finos, keep less well, though they are fairly sturdy, too. Just remember, the sweeter the wine, the longer it keeps after opening.

Stand the bottles up or lay them down; you don't have to keep the corks wet. But keep Sherry out of the sun. Though sunshine is important in the development of flavor in a Sherry, it can also ruin that flavor once the wine is in the bottle. Sherry bottles are brown for sun and light protection, but it is well to be a little cautious, too.

THOSE EENTSY LITTLE SHERRY GLASSES

They are cute, and if Great Aunt Martha has given you a set, use them, by all means. But people who love Sherry think that they are too small, and that there isn't nose room in them. The all-purpose, 8- or 9-ounce tulip-shaped wineglass is much more satisfactory, they contend. While the traditional Sherry glass must be filled almost full if you are to have more than a sip, the bigger glass is filled about a third full, offering you a nice drink of Sherry and plenty of room in which to capture that aroma within the glass.

WHEN AND WITH WHAT TO SERVE SHERRY

In Spain Sherry may be served throughout a meal, but Americans usually take it before and after, or in-between. Even so, there's no getting away from eating as one sips Sherry. It is a wine that seems to demand food, especially

At wine cellars in New York, Sherry ages in fifty-gallon white oak barrels in the solera (roof-top). The wine resides here for four years, and vintage and other required data are carefully stencilled on each barrel.

salty, spicy food. In Spain small appetizers known as *tapas* are brought forth with Sherry. They may be simply olives or salty almonds, rolled anchovies or plump shrimps. Or they may include fried squid and elaborate, highly seasoned hors d'oeuvres.

Cheese spreads and dips, smoked oysters or mussels, smoked salmon, clam mixtures, crab puffs (see recipe, page 174), all are good with Sherry when you are serving it at a Sherry (cocktail) party. Peppery salami, Virginia ham, smoked turkey or pheasant could be pleasant companions. Spicy, hot meat balls or fish bites with a hot sauce would be good.

If you aren't having a party, but simply wish to offer Sherry to a guest, salted nuts, cheese crackers, cubes of sharp cheese or simple cookies would be suitable accompaniment.

And, by the way, although the cocktail Sherries should be served cold, the sweet ones may be at room temperature, if you like.

HOLD A SHERRY WINE-TASTING

Two bottles of good Sherry, one from Jerez, one from New York or California, could inspire a wine-tasting. Cover the labels and let everybody guess which is the imported, which the American Sherry.

Or taste a series of Sherries from dry to sweet (never from sweet to dry, or your palate will never approve of the non-sweet ones!). You can learn a lot about Sherries this way.

Keep the accompaniments simple while you make comparisons—crackers or celery will remove the taste of one Sherry and prepare your taste buds for the next.

SHERRY IN COOKING

Sherry is the most versatile wine for cooking. It can flavor anything from the cheese dip to the sauce for dessert.

Soups, seafoods, poultry and meats can often be made more flavorsome by the judicious addition of Sherry. It is possible to use too much Sherry; the good cook is careful not to do so. Favorite seasoning tricks of chefs include the following:

Pour a tablespoonful of Sherry (any but a very sweet one) into a soup bowl before pouring the hot soup. Done at table, the fragrance engulfs the diner, whetting his appetite. Sherry is good in consommé, bisques and cream soups, chowders, bean and split pea soup.

Add two or three tablespoons of Sherry to a cream sauce for a fish or seafood dish, with or without mushrooms.

Baste a browning ham with a sweet Sherry. Or spread the ham with brown sugar, mustard and Sherry, mixed together.

Add a few tablespoons of Sherry to a veal stew or sauce for veal, or to almost any gravy.

Season chicken or turkey with Sherry, in broiler, on rotisserie, in skillet or casserole.

Pour as much as half a cup of Sherry into the pot of baking beans. Flavor beans out of a can with Sherry, too.

Sherried olives are wonderful. Drain the liquid from a can or jar of green, ripe or in-between olives, replace it with Sherry and chill for a couple of hours.

I'm sure you know about Sherried grapefruit—a tablespoon of Sherry, a tablespoon of brown sugar and a teaspoon of butter on a grapefruit half, then broil and enjoy as breakfast fruit or dessert.

There's no unbreakable rule about it, but I'd try to use the drier Sherries in seasoning entrees and appetizers, the sweeter ones for desserts and dessert sauces.

You'll find some deliciously Sherried dishes in the recipe collection.

PORT IS FOR OPORTO

The English, who have always influenced the Sherry and Madeira trade, have drunk Port for six centuries and were responsible for changing the character of this Portuguese wine. It was once a rather rough red wine; the English transformed it into what is known as a "generous" wine, one fortified with grape brandy to improve both flavor and keeping qualities. Port has an alcoholic content of around 20 per cent.

This highly prized, sweet wine is grown on steep slopes bordering the upper Doura River, in northern Portugal. Like the Sherry of its neighbor, Spain, Port is a blended wine as well as a fortified one. Usually, ten to fifteen grape varieties go into Port, although a rare vintage may be made of only one grape of a special year.

Port gets its name from the city of Oporto at the Doura's mouth, from whence it is shipped. While Port is not always red, it is almost always a sweet wine, and it has imitations wherever wines are grown. From New York, Ohio and California flow rivers of Port-type wines. They shouldn't really be compared with Portuguese Port.

Portuguese Ports are produced in these classifications:

Ruby Port, the deep red, full-bodied, fruity sweet beverage we think of when the name "Port" is mentioned.

Tawny Port, a mellower, less sweet wine which has lightened in color during a longer aging in wood. It is more highly prized by connoisseurs than ruby Port.

White Port, which in Portugal is made from white grapes alone instead of from a blend of white and colored grapes.

Vintage and *Crusted Port.* These are rare and expensive wines, the only Ports that improve in the bottle. They are often allowed to mature for twenty or thirty years, and during that time may develop a crust or deposit requiring careful decanting. Vintage Port bears a date on its label; recent vintage years are 1942, 1945, 1947, 1948, 1950, 1955 and 1960. These are wines to purchase in middle life, to enjoy in one's old age. They are wines traditionally purchased upon the birth of a son, to be opened at the time of his twenty-first birthday.

A very few California Ports will mature like this. How many Americans are patient enough to wait twenty years to drink a wine is a question.

American Port-type wines are invariably sweet, and come ruby, tawny and white. There are differences between these and true Port. A California tawny Port is tawny-colored not because it has matured longer than ruby Port in the cask, but because it is made from grapes less highly colored than those used in ruby Port. American white Ports usually are made from the same kinds of grapes as the red Ports, minus the skins that color the wine.

It is safe to say that none but high quality Portuguese Ports reach our shores. But some mighty indifferent Port-type wines are turned out domestically. On the other hand, some quite drinkable ones are available, and they are much less expensive than the imports.

HOW AND WHEN TO SERVE PORT

Port is a wine to serve with cheese or nuts. It is an after-dinner wine, a good one to bring forth in front of a crackling fire on an evening when the chill wind howls outside. There are those who think of Port as a man's wine, perhaps because of the strength of its alcoholic content.

Serve Port at room temperature in a glass big enough for your nose.

COOKING WITH PORT

Port can flavor the game sauce or baste the ham. It mixes with cheese, especially cheddar, to make an excellent spread. It may be used to flavor cakes, cookies and puddings, and it is a perfect partner for fruits. Pour Port over canned or fresh pears or peaches, strawberries or raspberries. Serve melon balls (honeydew, cantaloupe and others) in Port.

. . . AND MADEIRA'S FOR MADEIRA

"Have some Madeira, m'dear?"

The British have always loved the forceful wines of the charming island of Madeira, southwest of Portugal and not far from the coast of Morocco. In Revolutionary times we loved it, too, and why not, since it was almost the only wine available to Americans? Later, French and German wines seemed more to the taste of our countrymen. But now, perhaps, one may expect a revival of interest in Madeira, since American tourists are visiting the island, sampling its wines and coming back with taste buds attuned to its rather pungent flavor. Madeira is the Portuguese counterpart of Spain's Sherry. Yet it is not Sherry but a distinguished wine in its own right.

Like Sherry, Madeira is a fortified wine (about 19 per cent alcohol by volume), and like Sherry, it is "baked," but by a different method. It is given a sort of hothouse treatment. I have heard it said that American Sherries resemble Madeira more than Sherry because of the similarity of the heating process.

Like Sherry, Madeira is a wine blended from different vintages. Madeira can live longer than other wines. It can last more than a hundred years with undiminished quality. Anyone who possesses hundred-year-old Madeira might as well own the Mona Lisa—he has a treasure!

Wines grown in volcanic soil always assert themselves. Madeira's soil is volcanic, and the island basks in year-round sunshine, another factor influencing the grapes and the winemaking. Madeiras are named for the grapes from which they are made. There are four principal Madeiras; not all may be available at your wineseller's. Sometimes you'll find only one. But this country imports all four.

THE KINDS OF MADEIRA (*all named for their grapes*)

Sercial is pale to golden, nutty in flavor. The sercial grape, surprisingly, is the riesling of the Rhine, but in Madeira's climate, with Madeira's very different soil, this grape produces an entirely different wine. Sercial is the cocktail choice. Slightly chilled or served on the rocks, it is an excellent appetizer.

Verdelho is a medium-dry wine, an excellent all-purpose Madeira. It has rich golden color, good bouquet. It is often used to flavor soup or to accompany soup. "Rainwater" Madeira, of similar description, once was a type but now is a brand.

Bual or *Boal* is a dessert wine, probably the one most generally popular in all countries. It is a wine to serve in the afternoon or evening, and it has an affinity for fruit.

Malmsey, sweet, rich and luscious, with a fine bouquet, is considered the proper companion for cheese. This is the kind of Madeira you could keep for your great-grandchildren. The grapes for Malmsey are gathered when they are sun-dried and raisiny.

George, duke of Clarence, imprisoned for treason in the Tower of London in 1478, drowned himself in a butt of Malmsey, thereby adding to the romantic history of the wine.

The British have always dominated the Madeira wine

trade, although Madeira is a Portuguese island. They used to ship the wine to India and back a time or two "to mature it," but then found that it was tropical heat, not the shaking up of a sea voyage that aged the wine.

American wines labeled Madeira may be quite drinkable, but they cannot be compared with Madeira Madeira, m'dear.

OTHER FORTIFIED WINES

Malaga, a Victorian favorite, is a very sweet, dark Spanish wine made in the vicinity of Malaga, around the coastline to the east of Jerez de la Frontera.

Marsala is Sicily's generous wine. Grown in volcanic soil, it is a heavy wine, deep amber in color, and somewhat like Madeira. Marsala was developed by an Englishman late in the eighteenth century to create some competition for the popular Ports and Sherries of the time.

8. DESSERT WINES AND THE BUBBLY ONES

God, in His goodness, sent the grapes to cheer both great and small; Little fools will drink too much and great fools none at all.—Anonymous

Most of us begin our wine drinking with a sweet wine which has a more immediate appeal to the palate than a dry one. Dessert wines are the sturdy ones that keep on the pantry shelf after being opened. They include sweet Sherries and Port. They don't need to be stored on their sides. Except for vintage Port which always needs gentle treatment, they can take shaking around, temperature changes and like abuse.

Most dessert wines are fortified wines. Their fermentation has been halted at the proper point of sweetness with a dosage of pure grape brandy, often made from the same grapes as the wine. Their alcoholic content is around 20 per cent.

Most dessert wines aren't actually served with dessert, although they are good companions for pastry, fruit and cakes. Their most frequent appearances are in the afternoon or evening when they are brought out with a plate of cookies or a bowl of crunchy nuts. Occasionally they are served with ice cubes and sparkling water as summertime drinks, but more often they are poured from the bottle into the wineglass and served at room temperature. The glass usually is filled no more than a third full of dessert wine because of its strength and sweetness. A 2½-ounce portion is about average.

AMERICAN DESSERT WINES

California's dessert wines are of three general types: *Port*, *Muscatel* and *Tokay*. (Sweet Sherries are dessert wines, too, of course, but they are nevertheless classified as appetizer wines.) Most of these wines are grown in hot Southern California interior regions where the sun blazes long on the grapes.

With a few exceptions, California's Ports bear no resemblance to the Ports of Portugal. They are very sweet, fruity, heavy-bodied wines, about 19 to 20 per cent alcohol, and they are usually deep red. There are "tawny" Ports, also, often obtaining their tawny color from the grapes used rather than from long aging in the cask, as in Portugal.

White Port is a sweet, light-colored wine, not Port-like at all. Sometimes it is even "decolorized" to lighten its tone. There are some pleasant American white Ports, however.

While almost any grapes or combination of grapes may be used to make "Port" in California, there are a few serious vintners who plant Portuguese grapes, cultivate them carefully and use Portuguese methods for wines that are aged in the cask and then in the bottle. The best of these usually are labeled "Tinta Madeira" (a varietal) and "Tinta Port," and there are several vintage Ports. John Melville, in his *Guide to California Wines,* lists as outstanding the Ports of Almadén, Novitiate of Los Gatos, Buena Vista, Louis Martini, Richert and Sons, Guild Ceremony, Weibel and Ficklin. The last has been highly praised by connoisseurs. Like good Portuguese Ports, these wines may throw a sediment, and when they do, they should be poured carefully, or if necessary, be decanted.

Oceans of cheap red wines masquerade as Port.

The Muscatels are numerous. They are made from any of a number of muscat grape varieties, muscat of Alexandria being most common. All Muscatels have the characteristic flavor of the grape. Muscatels range in color from golden and dark amber to red. Sweetness varies somewhat, but all of the Muscatels are rich, heavy and flavorful.

Muscat de Frontignan, a varietal, is considered California's best. It is golden, perfumed and tastes strongly of its grapes. Black Muscat, a red Muscatel from muscat Hamburg grapes, is another good one. Aleatico is a red Muscatel made from aleatico grapes, a muscat variety. It shouldn't be confused with Italy's Aleatico, also a dessert wine from aleatico grapes. California Aleatico may be better.

Then there's Tokay which is a blend of wines with some Sherry in it. It is not as sweet as the Ports or Muscatels, and it bears no resemblance whatsoever to the famous Tokays of Hungary. It is not made from the tokay grapes which we eat in winter, although sometimes some of their juice may get into the blend. California Tokay is quite ordinary wine.

New York state makes some Muscatels from California juices. This process never works in reverse, for California bars grapes and juices from other states in its wine production.

There are also some pleasing Ports and white Ports from the Finger Lakes region in New York.

Many Concord grape wines come from eastern vineyards, including some sweetened with sugar and sucaryl. These are mostly sacramental and kosher wines, with the characteristic fruity flavor of Concord grapes. Although very sweet, they really aren't classed as dessert wines because they aren't fortified.

SEVERAL FAMOUS NON-FORTIFIED DESSERT WINES AND THEIR AMERICAN NAMESAKES

"Sauternes is the finest white wine in the world!"

"No dessert wine anywhere can match Sauternes!"

Have you read such statements, and have you wondered what is the difference between French Sauternes and American Sauterne without the final *s*? And haven't you wondered what dry Sauterne and Haut (oh) Sauterne may be?

The simple truth is that in borrowing the name of the magnificent French wine for some very ordinary white wines, some early California winemaker dropped the *s*, probably taking it for a plural. Sauternes is the name of a town in the Bordeaux region of France, and only the fragrant lemon-gold nectar produced there is *really* Sauternes. We are beginning to call the best of our "Sauterne" wines by their grape names, such as *Sweet Semillon* or *Sweet Sauvignon Blanc*. Those grapes are the Sauternes varieties. But there is a difference between our wines and the French ones, even when ours too are sweet: the "noble rot" or "noble mold."

"Noble rot," called *pourriture noble* (poo-ree-teur *nawb*-l) by the French and *edelfäule* by the German winemaker, is one of the most interesting diseases of grapes. It is interesting because it is so desirable. Like the mold in blue-veined cheeses, it produces a distinctive and precious product.

Noble rot is a fungus which attacks grapes in the Sauternes and Rhine districts, causing the grape-berries to shrink, shrivel, and become raisiny as they lose water content. At the same time, there is a concentration of grape sugar in the ripe berries. They are often picked grape by grape, yielding flavorsome nectar which produces fine and expensive wines.

Foggy mornings, hot, sunny daytimes, and a late, warm autumn are the bringers of noble *pourriture*, but wine from such grapes is always a gamble for the vintner. A frost can wipe out his chances of success overnight.

If he harvests his grapes early enough in the season to be safe, he can perhaps make 2,400 liters of wine of good quality. If he waits for the noble rot to shrivel the grapes, and if the weather co-operates, he may obtain only 400 liters of wine from the same vines. But it will be a marvelously rich wine, and it will command a great price. Day by day, in early autumn he must ask himself, "Shall I harvest now, or wait for a greater wine?" Who knows when frost will nip those shriveled berries and perhaps bring financial disaster?

Barsac, an equally sweet and fragrant wine, is blood sister to Sauternes, grown and bottled in neighboring Barsac.

The term Sauterne in California is a loose one taking in a great many white table wines, good, bad and indifferent. The best of them are varietals, named for their grapes. "Haut" Sauterne usually suggests a semi-sweet wine. There's a true story about a young woman who ordered Haut Sauterne from a wine list, not knowing the correct pronunciation of "haut." Her waiter, equally uninformed, brought her *hot* white wine!

While the French serve their Sauternes (the most famous of which is Château d'Yquem) with pastry, soufflés, cakes and puddings, they also sometimes serve it with fish, sweet as it is. Salmon, smoked salmon, trout and shellfish are among those for which this wine is suited. It is not served with blander fish.

American sweet Sauternes, Semillons and Sauvignons Blancs may be served with desserts or with seafoods.

TOKAY IN CALIFORNIA AND IN HUNGARY

The name is the same, but there the likeness ends. (For one thing, the Hungarian spelling is "tokaj.")

California Tokay is a blend of Port, Sherry and Angelica—not Portuguese Port or Spanish Sherry, you may be sure. Angelica is a very sweet wine made of raisin grapes which Tom Marvel, in his *Pocket Dictionary of Wines*, describes as "worth knowing in order to avoid."

Hungary's wine, though, is universally praised. It comes from the environs of a little village called Tokaj, where the soil is volcanic, imparting a fieriness to the wine. The grapes are the furmint variety, and the wine is made when they are fully ripe or overripe and touched by the noble rot.

The rarest of Hungarian Tokays is a wine that can live for a century or more.* It is called *Eszencia* (essence) or Imperial Tokay. Its grapes are not pressed; the precious nectar just oozes out under the weight of the grapes. The wine is fragrant and rich, but of relatively low alcoholic content.

Aszu Tokay, sometimes called Ausbruch and known as royal wine, is a little less sweet, also precious. It is made from a combination of ripe and overripe, *edelfäule*-touched grapes. To the ripe grape juice is added some of the oozings from grapes shriveled by the noble rot. The grapes with *edelfäule* are placed in thirty-pound baskets (*puttonyos*) and added to thirty-gallon casks of regular wines. The label of

* Julian Street, in *Wines*, mentions a newspaper account of the marriage of the president of Poland in 1933 which reported that toasts were drunk in 250-year old wine. "The wine, if good, could only have been Essence of Tokay, and the centuries old traditional friendship between Poland and Hungary would seem to support this conclusion."

the wine tells you how many puttonyos of the precious grapes have been added in numbers from 1 to 5. The higher the number, the richer and finer the wine, and the higher the purchase price.

Wines like these are fun to know about, but the Tokay we are most likely to find and to be able to pay for is called *Szamorodni.* Szamorodni can be a dry wine in years when there aren't any overripe grapes; it is sweet in other years. Szamorodni can last a good twenty years.

And now you know the difference between Tokay and Tokaj.

THE NOBLE ROT IN GERMANY

The German equivalent of France's great Sauternes and Hungary's renowned Tokay is *Trockenbeerenauslese.* If that sounds like an impossible mouthful, let's break it down. *Trocken* means dried, *beeren* means berries (individual grapes), and *auslese,* selected. Pronounce it trocken-beeren-ows-laysuh. For this rare, expensive ($40 a bottle, perhaps!) wine the grapes must be threaded with the noble rot. It is a wine for which conditions are right only several times in a century. Trockenbeerenauslese is so rich and sweet that it is served as a liqueur rather than as a dessert wine.

The late Guy Armanetti, Chicago wine dealer, told of a customer who used to come into his wine shop regularly and who always wistfully eyed a bottle of Trockenbeerenauslese. "*Some day,*" he would say, "*some day* I am going to have money enough to buy that bottle!"

Each week he'd come for his good, everyday wines. Each week he'd declare, "One of these days I'm going to be rich enough to buy that wine!"

At last the customer came for his Trockenbeerenauslese. The bills were counted out and the happy man went off triumphantly cradling the precious bottle. The

Armanettis were joyful, too. They could scarcely wait for a report on the experience of sipping one of the rarest wines in the world.

Back came the customer. Surprisingly he said nothing, just went about gathering his ordinary wines.

"How was it?" asked Armanetti, in great suspense.

"Oh, that!" said the man. "We didn't like it. It was too sweet!"

CHAMPAGNE IS THE CELEBRATION WINE

"Come quickly!" cried Dom Perignon, a Benedictine monk. "I'm drinking stars!"

The year was 1679, the place the abbey of Hautvillers in the valley of the Marne, and the monk, cellarer of the monastery, had just tasted a white wine which accidentally had undergone a secondary fermentation in the bottle. Thus was Champagne born. Or so goes the story.

Actually, records show, the stars already were in the wine. It was known as "devil's wine" for its mysterious habit of bursting out of the bottle in the spring. Dom Perignon's great discovery was how to keep the wine in the bottle by means of a cork instead of the crude seals used before his time. The monk was blind and possessed highly developed senses of smell and taste. He also discovered how to mix and blend the wines of different growths so that the best qualities of each contributed to the finished wine.

Champagne is a wine of around 12 per cent alcohol, blended from grapes of different years.* The grapes are the grapes of Burgundy, the pinot noir and two relatives, white pinot and pinot chardonnay. In the chalky soil of Cham-

* In the best years some "vintage" Champagnes are made from the grapes of that year only. They are expensive wines. Recent vintage years for French Champagnes are 1952, 1953, 1955, 1959, 1961 and 1962.

pagne the wine is very different from that of Burgundy, even with the Burgundy grape as its source. The Champagne district of France lies north and east of Paris along the Marne. The towns of Ay and Epernay and the city of Rheims are its heart and soul. Paris is a sparkling city by reason of its proximity, say the French.

When you visit Paris, you'll find that a one-day trip to Epernay and back will give you a fascinating look at how Champagne is grown and made. You may visit the old abbey of Hautvillers where Dom Perignon perfected this famous wine, and you'll be amazed at the miles and miles of wine cellars underlying the area.

HOW CHAMPAGNE IS MADE

The precious grape juices, after pressing, are placed in glass-lined tanks with the sugar needed for fermentation. Here they remain until spring, when the wines are "racked" to remove sediment, then blended with wines of other years for balance of flavor, bouquet and other qualities. Then, after a "dosage" of yeast culture and sirup, the wine is bottled and set away to age for three or four years, during which time it ferments, mysteriously at the time the vines flower, again at harvest, and a third time when the first fermentation of the new wine begins. Some winemakers believe that the phases of the moon determine these periods of fermentation.

During the fermentation, pressure builds up in the bottle. After the three or four years, the bottles are racked in a down-slanting position so that the sediment produced during the second fermentation may be collected. Each day they are turned an eighth of a turn by hand so that the deposit will not crust in one spot, and tilted slightly until at last they are vertical. After a few weeks of this turning and tilting, which must be done by hand, the bottles are ready for the disgorging operation. This removes the temporary cork with the sediment settled upon it, and replaces it with the permanent, wired-on cork.

I have seen the *degorgement* process four times: in Epernay in the cellars of Möet and Chandon, world's largest producers of Champagne; at the Taylor Wine Company in New York, largest American producers; and at Almadén Vineyards and Korbel, in California. In all these places the same method is used. The necks of the bottles are frozen where the sediment has settled. Corks are skilfully removed, permitting the frozen plug of settlings to shoot out under the pressure of the wine, then lost wine is quickly replaced with older wine, including another "dosage" which determines the degree of sweetness in the finished Champagne. After that, a compressed cork is set into the neck of the bottle and wired down. Now the wine is ready for its metal cap and labels, and a final aging.

The dosage determines whether the wine will be "brut" (very dry), "extra dry" (dry), or "demi sec" (fairly sweet). The popular preference is brut. "Doux" (doo) or sweet Champagne seldom is made any more. A few companies make a "*nature*" Champagne with no dosage at all. Korbel has an excellent one.

THE CHARMAT OR BULK PROCESS OF MAKING CHAMPAGNE

The process just described is the only one permitted in France. But in the United States it is possible to take short cuts which do not involve so much hand labor. Bulk process Champagne can be sold cheaper.

The method is called Charmat, for its inventor, and it involves secondary fermentation in a closed tank, after which the wine is filtered and bottled under pressure. Some California and eastern Champagne producers use both methods, selling the bulk Champagne at lower prices.

Other companies, such as Meier's Wine Cellars in Ohio and Christian Brothers in California, use only the bulk method. The label will tell you if the bulk method was used.

The most expensive wines and usually the top quality Champagnes are made by the French process, but the others often are quite good.

WHY CHAMPAGNE IS EXPENSIVE

Champagne grapes are difficult to cultivate (American Champagnes are not made of the pinot grapes which legally are the only ones used in France, but other hard-to-grow varieties are likely to be best for the purpose!), and they have a low yield. A great deal of time and hand labor is involved in producing the best of them. And a third factor is the "tax on bubbles." Bubbly wines are unreasonably taxed in comparison with still wines, most wine producers and wine lovers agree.

RED, PINK AND ROSÉ CHAMPAGNES

Most of the red and pink Champagnes are made in this country. The French do make a sparkling Burgundy for Americans, but they do not use their best Burgundy wines for it, and it usually is inferior to American sparkling Burgundy, which is by our standards really red Champagne. Bulk process or secondary fermentation in the bottle may be used. The label will tell you.

Sparkling Burgundy is sweeter than Champagne and slightly more limited in its use. It is served as a table wine, with meats as a rule, while its pale and more aristocratic white wine cousin can be served throughout a meal, and at any time of day.

OTHER BUBBLING WINES

Italy's "Champagne"* is Asti Spumante, made of muscat grapes and sweeter than Champagne. Lacrima Christi and Nebbiolo Spumante are other Italian sparklers which are worth trying. Germany has some naturally sparkling Moselles and sends to market vast quantities of "Sekt," which in this country could be called Champagne.

There are some carbonated wines, also. Usually the bubbles do not last as long when a wine is artificially carbonated. California wines must be labeled "carbonated" or "effervescent" if they are not naturally sparkling. They cannot be called "sparkling."

GOOD CHAMPAGNE BUBBLES A LONG TIME

The best Champagnes show off small steady bubbles for a long time in the glass. The better to admire the bubbles, Champagne glasses are deep. The all-purpose glass is fine; the tall slim tulip Champagne glass is also much used.

Chill Champagne an hour in the refrigerator or fifteen minutes in an ice bucket. This advice goes for other bubbly wines as well.

HOW TO POP THE CORK

You don't want a big explosion that will shoot out wine as well as cork, so avoid shaking the bottle. Begin by removing the foil. With the bottle resting on the table, remove the wire fastener over the cork, keeping a thumb on the cork. Pick up the bottle, grasp the cork firmly and twist the bottle, not the cork, until the cork pops quietly but eloquently. Have a glass ready to catch any overflow of wine. Fill saucer or tulip Champagne glasses nearly full; fill the all-purpose glass not more than two-thirds full.

* The United States is the only country which calls its sparkling wines "Champagne," outside of France, and the Champagne district there is legally limited.

The best Champagnes have bubbles that last a long time. Champagne should be chilled for an hour in the refrigerator or for fifteen minutes in an ice bucket. The all-purpose wineglass is quite suitable.

CHAMPAGNE AND FOODS

The wine may be served any time, and is a favorite beverage for a wedding breakfast. Foods should be worthy of it. Wedding feast foods, including the cakes and sandwiches, cold turkey and ham and seafood salads often served, are excellent companions for this queen of wines. All of the foods that signify good living are appropriate—roast turkey, roast beef, broiled lobster, Dover sole, Virginia ham, to mention only a few.

Champagne is the wine for launching ships, christening babies, toasting brides. A toast to newlyweds is this one:

> Here's to the health of the happy pair!
> May good luck meet them everywhere,
> And may each day of wedded bliss
> Be always just as sweet as this.

A more frivolous Champagne toast is this one:

> Here's Champagne to our real friends,
> And real pain to our sham friends!

Frederick the Great brewed coffee with Champagne instead of water. Then he spoiled everything by stirring in mustard!

NAMES IN FRENCH CHAMPAGNE

Moët and Chandon makes the most Champagne. However, Mumm produces most of what we import. Other well-known names include Bollinger, Mercier, Krug, Pol Roger, Piper Heidsieck, Charles Heidsieck, Taittinger, Veuve Cliquot-Ponsardin, Roedérer, Pommery and Greno, Lanson and Irroy.

AMERICAN CHAMPAGNES

From California: Almadén, Beaulieu,* Cresta Blanca, B. Cribari and Sons, Cucamonga, Korbel, Hanns Kornell Cellars, Paul Masson, Martin Ray,* Weibel. Cook's Imperial, a California Champagne, is a Midwestern best-seller.

Christian Brothers and United Vintners produce Charmat process Champagnes only, while Cucamonga and Weibel make bottle-fermented and Charmat process as well.

From New York and New Jersey: Gold Seal and Charles Fournier labels, Taylor and Great Western labels (two separate lines of Champagne; both companies are owned by Taylor), Renault (bottle fermented and Charmat).

From Ohio: Meier's Wine Cellars, Charmat process.

* Limited production of high quality wine.

9. OTHER WINES

When a man drinks wine, he begins to be better pleased with himself.—Plato

EVERYTHING'S ROSÉ NOW

Rosé, the most versatile wine in the world, is also the easiest to appreciate. Usually, it's love at first sip.

The beautiful pink color is achieved by letting the skins of black grapes remain in the fermenting wine just long enough to produce the color wanted. Rosé has the freshness of white wines and some of the crisp dryness of reds. It is always served cold, and goes with any food.

Rosé is a perfect wine to serve with shellfish (the Portuguese produce a Rosé which they call *Lagosta,* the lobster wine). It is a wine to accompany turkey with chestnut or sausage or oyster stuffing; barbecued chicken done on the back yard grill; roast veal; pork chops; baked ham. Scrambled eggs, cold cuts and potato salad and casserole meals are made more enjoyable with Rosé, which is even a wine one may chill, pour into a vacuum jug and carry along to a picnic.

The fruity pink wine is an excellent summertime re fresher, by itself, with ice or ice and soda, mixed with lemonade or in a punch (see pages 154 and 155). It may be used in cooking as you'd use either a white or red wine, but more particularly it suits fish, seafood, chicken and spicy dishes such as curry. Alcoholic content is about 12 per cent.

All of these charms and virtues are available at modest cost, around $2 a bottle at most, except for some of the imports.

The quality of a Rosé is often judged by how closely it resembles Tavel Rosé, made from grenache grapes grown in the vicinity of Tavel, France, near Avignon in the Rhône valley. "Tavel," the connoisseur will say, "is the best pink wine in the world." It is good, all right, but I think that several of our California Rosés match it.

The northern coastal counties of California offer the climate suited for the development of the grape aristocrat known as grenache. A few vintners are willing to toil long, hard and lovingly to produce a quality wine from these grapes, which they label Grenache Rosé. It is a varietal wine, so labeled, if it is made of 51 per cent or more from the one grape variety; but most are 85 to 100 percent.

Other varietals include Gamay (the most common), Cabernet, Grignolino, Zinfandel and even, rarely, Pinot Noir, very choice when you can find it. One producer makes four varietal Rosés. The grape in each case influences the taste, but all are dry, fresh, light-bodied wines, pleasing and pretty. In New York there's a Seibel Rosé, a 100 per cent varietal from a French hybrid grape. It has an assertive bouquet and taste.

And to think that little more than twenty years ago

there were no pink wines at all produced in the United States!

In Bordeaux, where red wines live on for years, improving as they mature in the bottle, I sampled a thirty-year-old Rosé which was deep rose in color, and still delicious. But Rosés do not ordinarily grow old gracefully. They need to be drunk young, before their second birthday. After that there may be unattractive color and flavor changes. Buy Rosé wines to drink now, not to put away.

We import, in addition to Tavel, Rosé d'Arbois, Rosé d'Anjou and Côtes de Provence Rosé wines from France. The wines from Provence usually carry the vineyard name, preceded by "domaine," "clos" or "chateau," for example, "Château Ste. Roseline," an excellent pink wine from Provence, grapes for which are crushed only by their own weight. After their juices have been thus gently expressed, the grapes are sent elsewhere to be completely crushed and used for pink wine of lesser quality.

We import some pink wines from Italy and several from Portugal, including a "crackling" (carbonated) Rosé known as Lancer's Crackling. Some naturally-fermented-in-the-bottle sparkling Rosé is made in California. It is likely to be sweeter than the other Vins Rosés. Novices especially may enjoy it.

There are cheap pink wines, usually on the sweet side, made by mixing red and white wines, and there are some others for which red and white grapes are used. But a true Rosé wine is made from black grapes under carefully controlled fermentation, and usually is so superior as to announce its quality at first sip.

When in doubt, choose Rosé, the fresh and friendly, go-with-everything wine. It is a man's wine as well as a woman's. Only the color would lead anyone to call it "feminine." Ladies love it, but so do men—at the club with a filet of beef, or on the curb in a lunch bucket!

VERMOUTH, THE APERITIF WINE

Vermouth, it is commonly understood, is something to put into a martini or manhattan. If you are mixing martinis, you reach for the dry French Vermouth with one hand and a bottle of gin with the other; if manhattans are preferred, you grab for the Italian sweet Vermouth and the rye whiskey. Many long arguments have not determined how much Vermouth to put into either cocktail, but nobody questions the necessity of Vermouth.

Not all cocktail sippers know that Vermouth is a wine, an "aromatized" wine, an "aperitif" (appetizer) wine, one based on a blend of white wines flavored with forty or more herbs, spices and peels. The alcoholic content is between 15 and 20 per cent.

Vermouth was born in Torino, Italy, some authorities say, in the year 1786. Torino lies in the northwestern part of Italy, in the foothills of the Alps, among the meadows of the Piedmont region. It was there that white wines made from moscato grapes were first infused with herbs and set to age in casks. Or was this "birth" only a renaissance? Other wine scholars deny that Vermouth is that modern. They trace it back to the herbal wines which the ancient Greeks and Romans used as medicines.

Wormwood, myrrh and aloes were flavorings the Romans infused in their wines. Wormwood and aloes are used today in Vermouths, along with orange peel, mint, gentian, coriander, cinnamon, cardamom, thyme, angelica and quinine, which lends a pleasing bitterness. The name Vermouth comes from the German word for wormwood—*wermut*. Each producer of Vermouth has his own formula, which may be centuries old and often is a closely guarded secret.

The line of distinction between French and Italian Vermouths is blurring, now that France makes some sweeter Vermouths and Italy some drier ones. Many Californians and some New York vintners make Vermouth in dry, intermediate and sweet types. The better names in domestic wines usually offer good quality—greatly improved over those that first appeared after World War II shut off the French and Italian supply.

You should know that Vermouths are somewhat unstable. After a bottle has been opened for a few days or weeks, the flavor may change due to the effect of air on the various seasoners. Many authorities suggest half-bottles for this reason.

Winesellers tell me that the preference in martinis has been changing, that instead of Vermouth playing a very minor role in the martini pitcher, the trend is toward more Vermouth and less gin. Vermouth makes an excellent before-dinner drink, alone or on the rocks. Either dry or sweet Vermouth is good this way; some people blend the two kinds. Vermouth may also be served with ice, soda and a twist of lemon. Occasionally sweet Vermouth and dry Sherry are combined half and half, and are served cold or on the rocks as an appetizer.

Vermouth is just beginning to be used in cooking, and seems to suit the appetizers and soups best. It is good in fish dishes, too. Substitute Vermouth for Sherry in a cheese dip or a cream soup. I think you'll like the unusual, enigmatic flavor. Substitute Vermouth for white wine in fish dishes, now and then. The results often are intriguing. But use a light hand with Vermouth; it is pungent seasoning.

Other European aperitif wines which may be used like Vermouth include the French Byrrh (pronounced "beer," which is rather confusing), Dubonnet (Dew-bow-*nay*) Chambraise and St. Raphael, and the Italian Positano and Carpano Punt e Mes. Most of these are flavored with quinine, and some are quite bitter.

American "natural flavor" wines fit into this category and include such names as Thunderbird, Golden Spur and Silver Satin (see page 48).

AND THEN, THERE'S RETSINA

The first taste of Greek Retsina (Ret-*see*-nah) wine comes as a shock. "It tastes like medicine!" "*Turpentine!*" "Good heavens, it's *spoiled!*"

Those were some of the comments I heard at a small wine-tasting of Greek wines. Resin-flavored wine has been enjoyed by the Greeks for centuries. The Greeks were the earliest planters of the vine, and they stored their wines in beautiful jugs called *amphorae*, which often were lined and sealed with pitch. Some Greek wines also were exposed to the spicing of peppers, cloves and aromatic gums, which were used as preservatives and for medicinal purposes.

In modern Greece, resinated wine is preferred, and some is shipped to our shores. I will say that second and third tastes of Retsina are less startling. In time one might get used to it. Modern Greece is distinctly "in" these days as a tourist lure. Its food is interesting, and its wines are becoming more familiar. And not all of them taste of pine pitch.

One pleasant dry white wine, Pallini, which comes in a tall slim Rhine wine bottle, is exceedingly good with fish or chicken, or just to sip, well-chilled, in the afternoon. Hymettus is an amber-colored dry wine worth knowing, and there are good Rosés and reds for the dinner table.

There are a good many sweet wines from Greece including Moscato de Rhodes, Muscat of Samos, beloved of Lord Byron, and Mavrodaphne, which somewhat resembles Port. All of these are fortified wines, up to 20 per cent in alcoholic content.

MAY WINE IS FRAGRANT, TOO

May wine is the essence of springtime. It is traditional in some parts of Germany and Austria to celebrate the coming of spring with a "maibohle," white wine flavored with the spring flower known as *waldmeister* or sweet woodruff. The first wild strawberries of spring go into the wine bowl, too. May wine is imported from Germany, but it is also made by a few California wineries. You may also make your own, if you can find the *waldmeister*, by steeping it in white wine and adding ice and strawberries.

This somewhat sweet, refreshing, flowery wine should always be served chilled, and it is not May wine unless it has strawberries and perhaps even violets floating on the surface.

10. WINE MAKES FOOD TASTE BETTER

Wine whets the wit, improves its native force, and gives a pleasant flavour to discourse.—John Pomfret

Cooking with wine is not new. Our first First Lady, Martha Washington, was famous for the foods she served; many of them were seasoned with wine. But Martha Washington did not invent wine cookery. She was following a tradition almost as old as wine itself. No one knows who "invented" wine cookery. The practice is so completely natural that it didn't have to be invented. It just happened, possibly when some early man, goatskin of wine in one hand, turned the ox on the spit and suddenly decided to give it a bath of wine.

It is astonishing what wine can do to enhance the flavor of foods and add to their appeal to the olfactory senses. After cooking veal chops, for example, pour a little white wine into the skillet, let it bubble and capture all the good meat drippings, then pour this "sauce" over the chops. *Abracadabra!* they've been transformed into a divine delicacy, pleasing the nose as much as the tongue.

Make a simple cream sauce for crabmeat or shrimps, or possibly for chicken. Then add a few tablespoons of California Sauterne or Chablis, tuck in the seafood and taste something exceedingly delectable!

As a general rule, use the wine that is the natural partner for the food you are seasoning. Add Burgundy to the beef stew or hamburger mixture, poach the fish in Rhine wine, pour Port or Muscatel over the fruit compote.

There are some famous exceptions—though not many—to the custom of cooking red wines with red meats, white wines with white meats. Red wine is used with chicken in the famous cacciatore; red wine makes the *marchand du vin* (merchant of wine) sauce for halibut or sole.

HOW MUCH WINE TO USE?

When you haven't a recipe to guide you, keep these proportions in mind:

1 tablespoon of wine per cup of sauce or soup.
¼ cup wine to season braised meats for four people.
½ cup wine for a beef stew.
As much as 2 cups wine for a marinade or to baste a ham or a roast during cooking.

DO YOU USE THE BEST WINES IN COOKING?

I wouldn't use any rare or expensive wine for cooking purposes. But most cooks who flavor with wines insist that if a wine is not good enough for drinking, it is not good enough for cooking. There's no such thing as a "cooking Sherry," they'll tell you. "Cooking" Sherry is a relic of prohibition and used to be salted so that it could not be consumed as wine. Some "cooking" Sherry still is made in New York.

It is salted "so chefs will put the wine into the food instead of drinking it," I'm told.

Wine changes as it blends with the dish it seasons. First the alcohol cooks away. Then other chemical changes take place. The longer the dish is cooked with the wine in it, the greater the change.

California cooks insist that we should accompany a wine-flavored dish with more of the wine used in preparing it. French cooks disagree. Because the wine is transformed, the original beverage may be quite unsuitable to accompany the food it flavors, they tell us. They choose a wine to complement the flavor of the finished dish.

So! Do as you wish. Serve the same wine or another. You'll have good authority for whichever course you choose.

Many excellent books on the subject of wine cookery have been published. I do not wish to compete with them. But any book which introduces its readers to wines and wine lore should also show them how wines can add charm and subtle seasoning to food. Perhaps this collection of what I consider very special, very "gourmet" recipes will inspire a few good cooks to seek out some of these cooking-with-wine volumes for further experimentation. A list will be found on page 258.

Good old versatile Sherry is almost anybody's favorite wine for flavoring food. I have tried not to choose a disproportionate number of Sherried dishes, but even so, Sherry stands out.

You can adventure pleasantly into the forests of wine cookery with just three bottles:

a Rhine wine, Chablis or Sauterne (California)
a Burgundy, Claret or other red table wine
a Sherry, either homegrown or imported

Keep the Sherry on a shelf in your pantry or cupboard; keep the white and red wines in the refrigerator after opening, and use them within a week or so, even if you have to *drink* your "cooking" wines!

RECIPES

PUNCHES AND WINE DRINKS

CHAMPAGNE PUNCH

(75 punch glasses, or 3 servings each for 25 persons)

For a wedding, freeze strawberries in a ring mold of ice to float in the punch bowl.

- Sliced strawberries
- ½ bottle each: Curaçao, Cognac, Maraschino Cordial
- 2 bottles Sauterne or Rhine wine
- 4 jiggers Grenadine (¾ cup)
- 2 bottles Champagne
- 2 quarts sparkling water

Place a large block of ice in a punch bowl and slice fruit over it. Add liqueurs, Sauterne and Grenadine. Pour in Champagne and sparkling water last, stirring gently.

LAKE KEUKA PUNCH
(for 10)

Choose New York state wines or you'll not have a Lake Keuka punch!

1 bottle extra dry Champagne
1 bottle sparkling Burgundy
1 bottle Sauterne
1 package frozen strawberries
2 teaspoons grated lime rind
Juice of 1 large lime

Chill wines. Combine berries and lime rind and juice, and simmer together for 10 minutes. Strain and cool, then pour over ice in a punch bowl. Add wines just before serving.

RHINE WINE AND CHAMPAGNE PUNCH
(36 servings; for 12 people)

For a patio party in summer, this punch is perfect.

About 1 pound fresh pineapple, peaches or strawberries
Sugar
3 bottles Rhine wine
1 bottle Champagne
¼ cup Cognac
¼ cup Curaçao

Slice fruit and place with sugar to taste in a large bowl or jug. Add the Rhine wine and leave for an hour. Turn mixture into punch bowl over a block of ice and add Champagne, Cognac and Curaçao. Stir gently. Serve with a slice of fruit in each glass.

SANGRIA
(for 3 or 4)

This is the sangria served in the Hotel Reina Cristina at Algeciras, Spain.

- 1 bottle red Rioja wine (or another red table wine)
- 2 tablespoons sugar
- 4 slices lemon
- 4 sliced peaches, fresh or canned
- Ice and sparkling water

Put everything into a big glass pitcher, stir vigorously and serve in wineglasses.

CHILEAN SANGRIA
(8 servings; serve to 4)

In Chile as in Spain, the wine punch is served at table with food.

- 1 cup sugar
- 2 cups water
- 1 orange, sliced thin
- 2 limes, sliced thin
- 1 bottle Chilean red or white wine

Boil sugar and water 5 minutes and while hot, add orange and lime slices. Let stand 4 hours or more. In a glass pitcher place about 12 ice cubes, 6 each of the soaked orange and lime slices and ½ cup of the syrup. Then add the wine. When you serve the punch, put 2 slices of fruit into each glass and serve from the pitcher.

Sangria

WEDDING PUNCH
(about 36 4-oz. servings; allow 2 or 3 apiece)

Here's an easy, beautiful and delicious celebration drink.

4 (6 oz.) cans frozen lemonade or limeade concentrate
1 quart fresh sliced ripe strawberries, lightly sugared
2 quarts sparkling water
Ice ring or ice cubes
2 quarts Champagne, Rhine wine, Sauterne or May wine

Mix the frozen concentrates with water as directed on the cans. Add strawberries and keep chilled until serving time. Add sparkling water and pour over ice ring or ice cubes in a large punch bowl. Add well-chilled wine, and stir gently before serving in punch cups. See that each serving has a slice of strawberry in it.

• • • • • • • • • • • • • • • • • • • •

ROSÉ WINE PUNCH WITH SHERBET
(50 to 60 servings for 20 to 30 persons)

The sherbets make this punch fluffy and frothy.

¾ cup granulated sugar
1 cup water
1 can frozen concentrated lemon juice
3 cans frozen concentrated orange juice
2 quarts sparkling water
3 bottles Rosé wine

ROSÉ SPARKLE PUNCH
(6 quarts, before dilution by ice; plenty for 20 to 24)

This is one of the prettiest and most popular of all punches.

4 (12 oz.) packages frozen sliced strawberries, thawed
1 cup sugar
4 bottles California Rosé wine
4 (6 oz.) cans frozen lemonade concentrate
2 large bottles sparkling water, chilled

In a bowl combine strawberries, sugar and 1 bottle of the wine. Cover and let stand at room temperature 1 hour. Strain mixture into a punch bowl. Add frozen lemonade concentrate, stir until completely thawed. Add remaining bottles of wine; pour in sparkling water. Add a block of ice or a tray of ice cubes. *Suggested garnish*: floating gardenias.

• • • • • • • • • • • • • • • • • • • •

1 bottle (8 oz.) maraschino cherries and juice
2 oranges, sliced thin
1 lemon, sliced thin
1 quart orange sherbet
1 quart lemon sherbet

In a large punch bowl, stir sugar into water until sugar dissolves. Combine juices, sparkling water and wine. Add cherries and juice and pour over syrup. Place large block of ice or ice cubes in a bowl and stir the mixture thoroughly. Float sliced fruit and drop in sherbets, whole or in scoops.

MALMSEY MULL
(about 10 servings, offering seconds to 5 people)

Defrost noses and toeses with this winter body-warmer.

1 navel orange, studded with cloves
1 bottle Malmsey Madeira
¼ cup apricot brandy
1 cup boiling water
½ cup sugar (or to taste)
Pinch of ginger

Bake the orange in a 350 degree oven for an hour. Heat Madeira and brandy with the baked orange until hot. Do not boil. Dissolve ginger and sugar in boiling water, add and stir gently. Serve in mugs or punch cups.

MULLED CLARET
(10 servings; for 5)

After skiing all day, here's the best way to relax!

½ cup sugar
1½ cups water
Peel from ½ lemon
10 whole cloves
1 stick cinnamon, broken up
¼ cup Curaçao or brandy
1 bottle Claret (or other red table wine)

Boil for 10 minutes the sugar, water, lemon peel (only the yellow part) and spices. Strain, add Curaçao or brandy, if used, and wine. Heat gently. Do not boil. Serve in mugs, glasses or punch cups. Sprinkle with nutmeg or use cinnamon sticks for muddlers.

JELLIED WINE SOUP
(4 to 6 servings)

A marvelous appetite-whetter. Serve it with cheese straws or tiny cheese crackers.

- 3 cups consommé, bouillon or well-seasoned chicken broth
- 2 tablespoons plain gelatin
- 1 cup Sherry, Sauterne, Port or Madeira

Soften gelatin in a little of the cold consommé, dissolve over hot water and mix with remaining consommé and wine. Chill until firm. Serve in bouillon cups. Break up the jelly with a fork before serving and garnish with sour cream or whipped cream. *Forget the gelatin sometimes* and serve the soup hot with 1 avocado, diced fine, added at the last minute.

WINE FRUIT SOUP
(6 servings)

Hot or cold, this first course is appetizing.

1 tablespoon cornstarch
¾ cup sugar
1 cup water
2-inch stick of cinnamon
¼ teaspoon mace
¼ teaspoon nutmeg
3 slices lemon
2 cups Claret, Burgundy, Cabernet or Rosé
2 cups rhubarb or strawberries, cut fine

Combine cornstarch and sugar. Add water and cook, stirring constantly, until mixture is thickened and smooth. Add spices, lemon slices, wine, and rhubarb or berries. Cook 5 minutes. Serve either piping hot or well-chilled, accompanied by water crackers.

• • • • • • • • • • • • • • • • • • • •

OXTAIL SOUP
(6 servings)

There's a lot of flavor in that steer's tail!

1 pound oxtail joints, floured
3 tablespoons oil
1 carrot, diced
1 medium onion, chopped fine
6 cups water
1 small bay leaf

Wine Fruit Soup

• • • • • • • • • • • • • • • • • • •

1 cup chopped celery
1 tablespoon barley
1 teaspoon salt; ½ teaspoon pepper
½ cup red table wine
2 tablespoons minced parsley

Brown meat in oil on all sides. Add carrot, onion and water, plus remaining ingredients except wine and parsley. Cover and simmer 3 hours. Remove meat from bones. Return meat to broth, add wine and serve with parsley.

POTATO SOUP WITH WINE
(4 servings)

Homemade soup isn't half as much trouble as you think, and it is *so* good!

2 slices bacon, cut fine
2 onions, chopped
4 medium potatoes, diced
2 bouillon cubes in 3 cups hot water
1 bay leaf
2 tablespoons chopped parsley
2 cups milk or milk and cream
½ cup white table wine
Salt, paprika

Cook bacon, add onions and cook until yellow. Add potatoes, bouillon, bay leaf. Cook until potatoes are tender. Stir in parsley, milk, wine. Adjust seasonings and serve with croutons.

Gourmet's touch for chops: dip pork or veal chops in Sherry, then coat with egg and crumbs, brown and braise as usual.

SALADS

AVOCADO-LIME MOUSSE
(6 servings)

A trite phrase, "out of this world," describes it, says a friend of mine.

- 1 package lime-flavored gelatin
- ½ cup hot water
- ½ cup Muscatel or white Port wine
- ¼ cup mayonnaise
- ½ cup heavy cream, whipped
- 1 tablespoon lime juice
- ½ teaspoon onion juice
- ½ teaspoon salt
- 1 cup finely diced avocado
- ½ cup finely diced celery
- 1 tablespoon grated green pepper
- Greens
- Orange or grapefruit sections

Dissolve gelatin in hot water and wine (don't *boil* wine!). Chill until slightly thickened. Beat until frothy; blend in mayonnaise, whipped cream, lime juice, onion juice and salt. Fold in avocado, celery and green pepper. Chill in oiled 1 quart ring mold until firm. Unmold on greens, garnish with citrus fruit sections and serve with French dressing.

MOLDED MELON BALL SALAD

(10 to 12 servings)

This mid-summer beauty may be made with 2 packages of lemon gelatin, but it will be sweeter.

- 2 tablespoons (envelopes) plain gelatin
- 1½ cups pineapple juice
- 1 cup melon juices (drain melon balls well)
- 1 cup sweet white wine
- 4 cups small melon balls (honeydew, cantaloupe and watermelon)

Soften gelatin in ½ cup cold pineapple juice for 5 minutes. Dissolve in remaining boiling pineapple juice. Add melon juice. Chill until partially thickened, stirring the mixture over ice cubes to hasten the chilling. Pour a thin layer of the thickened gelatin mixture into a 2 quart ring mold. Arrange a few melon balls to make a design in the gelatin. Chill until firm. Mix remaining balls with gelatin and fill mold. Chill until firm. To serve, unmold on salad greens or galax leaves. Serve with whipped cream and mayonnaise, equal parts. *I sometimes scatter* fresh blueberries among the melon balls. The contrast in color is lovely.

• •

POTATO SALAD WITH WHITE WINE

(4 or more servings)

There's remarkable flavor here for such a simple mixture.

- 8 small new potatoes, cooked in jackets
- ½ cup white table wine
- ½ bunch young onions, with tops, sliced

PARTY CHERRY MOLD
(8 servings)

When fresh sweet cherries are in season, substitute them for the canned fruit.

- 2 packages cherry-flavored gelatin dessert
- 2 cups boiling water and cherry juice
- 1 cup Port
- 1 No. 2½ can black sweet cherries, pitted, well-drained
- 1 3-oz. package cream cheese
- Pecan halves

Dissolve gelatin in boiling water and cherry juice and cool. Add Port. Chill until mixture begins to thicken. Spoon a little of the mixture into the bottom of your mold. Arrange in it cherries stuffed with cream cheese and pecans. Roll cream cheese into little balls to stuff the cherries, and top each ball with a pecan. Arrange nut-side down in the mold. Chill until firm. Then carefully spoon in the rest of the thickened gelatin, adding the other cherries which needn't be stuffed. Chill until firm.

• • • • • • • • • • • • • • • • • • • •

- ¼ cup salad oil
- 3 tablespoons tarragon vinegar
- 1 tablespoon sugar
- Salt, pepper
- 3 tablespoons minced parsley

Peel and slice potatoes while warm, moisten with the wine and add other ingredients. Mix lightly and chill several hours.

HOT POTATO SALAD WITH WINE
(4 to 6 servings)

This could become one of your favorite dishes.

- 4 to 6 medium-sized potatoes
- 4 slices bacon
- 2 tablespoons flour
- ¾ cup white table wine
- ¼ cup water
- 1 tablespoon instant onion (or ¼ cup chopped fresh onion)
- 1 teaspoon prepared mustard
- 1 tablespoon wine vinegar
- Salt, pepper
- 3 hard-cooked eggs
- ¾ cup thinly sliced celery

Cook potatoes in boiling salted water until tender. Drain, peel and dice them into a heated bowl. Meanwhile cook bacon until crisp, remove from pan and drain off all but 2 tablespoons fat. Blend in flour. Add wine, water, onion, mustard and vinegar, as well as salt and pepper to taste. Cook and stir until mixture has boiled and thickened. Dice eggs and add to potatoes with celery. Pour hot dressing over salad and mix lightly. Add crumbled bacon and extra salt, if needed. Serve while warm, or keep warm for serving over hot water.

 *Add a little Sherry to the deviled egg filling.*

SEAFOOD MOUSSE LOUISE
(10 to 12 servings)

This is a special-occasion molded salad, substantial and pleasing.

- 2 tablespoons (envelopes) unflavored gelatin
- ⅓ cup Sherry
- ½ cup boiling water
- 1¼ cups mayonnaise
- 1 cup chili sauce
- 1 tablespoon lemon juice
- ½ cup heavy cream, whipped
- 1 cup flaked cooked or canned crabmeat
- 1 cup finely cut (with scissors) cooked or canned shrimps
- 6 hard-cooked eggs, grated
- 4 oz. can chopped ripe olives, drained
- 2 tablespoons each, chopped parsley, pimiento
- 1 teaspoon each, grated onion, grated lemon peel, worcestershire sauce
- Dash tabasco, salt, pepper

Soften gelatin in wine for 5 minutes; dissolve in boiling water; cool. Blend mayonnaise, chili sauce, lemon juice. Add gelatin; fold in whipped cream. Add all remaining ingredients. Mix lightly but thoroughly. Turn into two 1 quart molds or 10 to 12 individual molds rinsed with cold water. Chill until firm. Unmold on crisp greens and garnish as you wish, possibly with slices of tomato and avocado, ripe olives and celery curls.

SHRIMP SALAD WITH WINE, IN TOMATOES
(4 servings)

A wine marinade subtly influences the flavor.

1½ cups cooked cleaned shrimps, cut in pieces
⅓ cup Sauterne, Chablis or Sherry
1 cup chopped celery
½ cup diced cucumber
3 hard-cooked eggs, chopped
1 teaspoon salt; little pepper
1 cup salad dressing
4 large tomatoes, hollowed, drained
Crisp salad greens

Add wine to shrimps and chill. Add remaining ingredients except tomatoes and greens, and mix well. Serve in tomato cups on a bed of salad greens.

FISH AND SEAFOOD

BROILED POMPANO A LA CAPRI

(4 servings)

"Delicious as the less criminal forms of sin," said Mark Twain of the pompano.

1 pompano (or turbot or Dover sole) split, boned
Salt, pepper
¼ cup butter, melted
¼ cup dry Vermouth
Fine dry bread crumbs
Grated cheddar cheese

Season fish with salt, pepper and broil until brown on each side, basting twice with the butter and wine. When almost done, sprinkle with crumbs and cheese and give the fish a minute more. Total cooking time shouldn't exceed 8 minutes.

BOUILLABAISSE
(8 generous servings)

This is a close copy of a prominent chef's recipe for the French specialty which can never be authentic without Mediterranean fish.

2 medium-sized lobster tails or 2 pounds lobster meat
1 pound small shrimps
2 perch
1 striped bass or red snapper (2 pounds)
¾ pound haddock fillets
1 cup butter (or olive oil)
¼ cup lemon juice
2 leeks, chopped
2 carrots, chopped
2 stalks celery, chopped
1 dozen shallots, chopped
2 pounds fresh tomatoes, peeled and chopped
½ teaspoon saffron, steeped in a little hot water and strained
½ teaspoon ground coriander
½ teaspoon thyme

• • • • • • • • • • • • • • • • • • • •

DEVILED SHAD ROE
(4 servings)

You might encounter such a dish in a fine restaurant, but it's easy at home.

2 shad roe, poached, cut in 1-inch pieces
1 teaspoon each, anchovy paste, turmeric
1 tablespoon prepared mustard
2 tablespoons butter
2 tablespoons or more Sherry

Salt, freshly ground pepper
¼ cup chopped parsley
1 cup white table wine
8 to 16 clams

Remove raw lobster tail meat from shells by cutting down the back of the shell with kitchen scissors or a sharp knife and forcing shell apart. Cut the tails into about 4 pieces each. Melt ½ cup of the butter in large skillet and add lobster tails. Let simmer gently 5 minutes. Add shrimps, leeks, carrots, celery and shallots. Add tomatoes and seasonings. Add wine and let cook gently while you prepare the other fish. Sauté the perch, filleted bass (cut in large pieces) and haddock fillets separately in the remaining butter. We bone our perch after cooking and put them into the stew, but they can be served whole as a garnish. Season these fish with lemon juice, salt and pepper, and put them in a hot tureen as soon as they are done. Add the lobster tail, shrimps, lifting them out of the sauce. Keep covered while you cook the sauce down rapidly for a few minutes. Cook clams (well-scrubbed, in their shells) gently in sauce 8 minutes. Add to stew. Adjust seasonings and pour sauce over fish. Garnish with slices of hard roll sautéed in garlic butter, and an extra sprinkle of parsley.

• • • • • • • • • • • • • • • • • • •

Toast
Watercress

To poach the roe, place it in cold water to cover, add 1 teaspoon salt, 2 slices lemon. Bring to simmering and cook gently 5 minutes for a small roe, 12 to 15 minutes for large one. Cut in 1-inch pieces. Make a paste of anchovy and remaining ingredients, and roll the roe in it (add more Sherry, if you need to). Arrange on toast and heat 5 minutes in a 450 degree oven. Garnish with watercress.

FISH TIMBALE RING WITH WINE SAUCE
(6 servings)

Halibut is my first choice for this delicacy, with fresh salmon next. The sauce is superb.

1 cup soft bread crumbs
¾ cup light cream or evaporated milk
¼ cup dry white wine
2 cups flaked, cooked or canned fish (halibut, salmon, tuna)
1 teaspoon minced onion
½ teaspoon each, salt, celery salt
¼ teaspoon pepper
3 eggs, separated

SAUCE:

¼ cup butter
¼ cup flour
1 cup cream or evaporated milk
½ cup water

• • • • • • • • • • • • • • • • • • • •

COQUILLES SAINT-JACQUES
(6 to 8 servings)

Scallops in wine with mushrooms are ambrosial fare.

2 pounds scallops
1 cup white table wine
½ pound mushrooms
6 green onions, chopped
¼ cup butter
2 tablespoons flour
2 tablespoons chopped parsley
Salt, few grains cayenne pepper

½ cup dry white wine
1 chicken or vegetable bouillon cube
2 tablespoons chopped parsley
½ teaspoon anchovy paste
1 teaspoon salt, a little pepper
Dash paprika
2 hard-cooked eggs, chopped fine
Chopped parsley for garnish

Soak bread crumbs in cream for 10 minutes; add wine, fish and onion; stir vigorously with a fork until well-blended. Add seasonings; stir in beaten egg yolks. Fold in stiffly beaten egg whites. Turn into greased 1 quart ring mold, place in a shallow pan of hot water, and bake at 350 degrees for 50 minutes or until firm. Let stand 5 minutes, then unmold on serving platter. *To make sauce,* melt butter and stir in flour; add liquids and cook, stirring constantly, until smooth and thickened. Add bouillon cube and stir until dissolved. Add parsley, anchovy and seasonings. Stir in eggs, pour over timbale ring and garnish with chopped parsley.

• • • • • • • • • • • • • • • • • • •

¼ cup cream
Buttered toasted bread crumbs

Simmer scallops in wine over low heat until cooked, a few minutes. Do not overcook. Drain and set aside the wine and broth from the scallops. Sauté mushrooms and onions in butter, remove mushrooms from pan and stir in flour. Add heated wine, parsley and seasonings, and stir to smooth sauce. Cut scallops in half with the grain and add to sauce with mushrooms. Add cream. Fill scallop shells; top with buttery crumbs. Set shells on a cooky sheet; bake at 350 degrees for 10 minutes or until hot. Slide under the broiler to brown tops.

Filet of Sole Bonne Femme

FILET OF SOLE BONNE FEMME
(3 to 4 servings)

Be careful not to overcook the sauce after adding the eggs. This dish is famous, and famously good.

6 filets of sole
2 tablespoons lemon juice
½ cup Chablis
¼ cup water
½ teaspoon salt
⅛ teaspoon freshly ground pepper
1 bay leaf
8 mushroom caps
2 tablespoons butter
3 tablespoons flour
2 tablespoons tarragon vinegar
¾ cup liquid from sole
½ cup cream
2 egg yolks, beaten

Arrange filets in baking dish, and pour the lemon juice, wine and water over them. Add salt, pepper and bay leaf. Cover the dish with aluminum foil and bake at 350 degrees for 15 minutes. Transfer sole to a hot serving dish. Sauté mushroom caps in butter. Remove from pan. Add to the butter the flour and vinegar, stirring until smooth. Add liquid from sole, cream and egg yolks and cook, stirring constantly until sauce is thickened. Remove from heat. Pour over sole and serve immediately, garnished with mushroom caps.

CRAB PUFFS
(makes 4 dozen)

You can fix these party goodies a day early, keep them chilled—then just heat at 350 degrees and serve.

- 2 packages pie crust mix
- ½ clove garlic minced
- 1 tablespoon finely chopped onion
- 3 tablespoons butter
- ¼ cup flour
- 1¾ cups cream
- ½ teaspoon salt
- ¼ cup Sherry or Madeira
- Tabasco sauce
- 6½ oz. can crabmeat, flaked
- 1 cup grated sharp process cheese
- 8 oz. package cream cheese
- 1 teaspoon worcestershire sauce
- ¼ cup cream
- 1 teaspoon each, paprika, dry mustard
- 1 egg

Prepare pastry as directed on package, rolling it to ⅛ inch in thickness. Cut pastry with fluted 1½ inch round cooky cutter. Press rounds into tiny muffin pans, making sure crust covers bottom and sides of cups. Prick pastry, then bake at 425 degrees for 8 to 10 minutes or until lightly browned. Cool. Sauté garlic and onion in butter until lightly browned; blend in flour, gradually add cream, stirring over moderate heat until mixture is smooth and thickened. Stir in salt, Sherry, drop or two of tabasco, and crab, mixing well. Spoon into pastry shells. Mix cheese, worcestershire sauce and cream until fluffy, then mix in paprika, mustard, egg. Spread over top of crab-filled cases, and broil until puffed and lightly browned, 3 to 4 minutes.

SAVORY DEVILED CRABS
(6 servings)

Makes a delicious luncheon with crunchy green salad and hot rolls.

- 2 packages frozen crab (6 oz. each), thawed, or
- 2 cans (6½ oz. each) crabmeat
- 2 hard-cooked eggs, chopped
- 1 cup mayonnaise
- 1 teaspoon each, minced onion, parsley, worcestershire, prepared mustard
- 2 teaspoons lemon juice
- ½ teaspoon salt
- ¼ cup Sherry
- 1 cup buttered crumbs

Mix crabmeat, wine, eggs, mayonnaise and seasonings. Fill 6 buttered ramekins and top with crumbs. Bake at 375 degrees for 15 to 20 minutes. Or bake in a casserole 25 minutes.

Glamour treatment for vegetables: frozen cooked, or canned artichoke hearts in cream sauce with white wine replacing some of the milk. Buttered crumb topping. Broil until bubbly. Try it on asparagus, too.

LOBSTER THERMIDOR

(4 servings)

This one's a rich, luxurious dish for people who don't count pennies or calories.

2 lobsters, split, or 4 lobster tails, cooked
¼ cup butter
⅓ cup flour
1 teaspoon each, salt, minced onion, dry mustard
¼ cup minced parsley
2 cups cream (or milk and cream)
½ cup Sherry
½ cup sautéed sliced fresh mushrooms or canned mushrooms
Pepper, cayenne pepper
2 tablespoons brandy
¼ cup grated Swiss cheese

Dice lobster meat. Melt butter, blend in flour and add seasonings. Add cream and cook and stir to smooth sauce. Add wine, mushrooms, pepper (better use white pepper, if you have it, to avoid black specks). Heat lobster in sauce, adding brandy, and fill shells. Top with cheese. Broil until bubbling and serve hot. *This dish* may be put together several hours early and refrigerated. To heat, place the lobster in a 350 degree oven for 15 minutes, then under broiler just until tinged with brown.

SEAFOOD SUPREME
(12 to 16 servings)

A white table wine may substitute for Sherry in this excellent, easy party dish.

½ cup butter or margarine
½ cup flour
2 cups chicken stock or canned broth or bouillon made from cubes
1 cup cream
6 oz. pimiento cream cheese
½ cup Sherry
Salt, pepper
4 cups diced cooked or canned lobster, shrimps, crabmeat (one or all three)
8 oz. can mushroom stems and pieces, drained

Melt butter and stir in flour; add chicken stock and cream; cook, stirring constantly, until mixture boils and thickens. Add cheese and wine; stir over low heat until cheese melts. Season with salt and pepper. Add seafood and mushrooms. Heat gently just until piping hot. Serve over mounds of hot cooked rice. The mixture may be prepared ahead of time and reheated just before serving in a chafing dish, the top of a double boiler, or over low heat.

For cooking you need a wine library of four bottles: Sherry, Port, a red table wine and a white table wine.

OYSTERS CHARLOTTE
(4 servings)

Oysters poached in wine are delicious, but consider the added attractions!

1 pint large oysters
1½ cups white table wine
1 tablespoon lemon juice
2 tablespoons butter
3 tablespoons flour
½ cup cream
½ teaspoon salt
⅛ teaspoon white pepper
⅛ teaspoon nutmeg
2 cups cooked shrimps or crabmeat, chopped
¼ cup fine dry bread crumbs

Poach the oysters gently in the wine and lemon juice until the edges begin to curl. Melt butter, stir in the flour, then the liquid in which oysters were poached. Cook, stirring constantly, until mixture thickens. Add cream and seasonings. Combine 1 cup of the sauce with the shrimps or crabmeat. Place in scallop shells or ramekins. Place several poached oysters on each portion and spoon sauce over oysters. Top with crumbs, dot with butter and brown quickly under broiler.

PANNED OYSTERS
(4 servings)

These take just a minute to fix; they make a good late supper.

1 pint large oysters
¼ cup butter
¼ cup dry white wine
Salt, pepper
Hot buttered toast
Lemon quarters, parsley

Drain oysters and heat in a skillet with butter until edges begin to curl. Add wine, salt and pepper, plus a dash of worcestershire sauce, if you wish. Bring to simmering. Serve on hot toast and garnish with lemon and parsley. These are "pan roast" oysters if you heat everything in a baking dish at 400 degrees for 10 minutes.

BROILED SHRIMPS WITH WHITE WINE
(4 to 5 servings)

Scrumptious and so easy!

2 pounds raw shrimps, shelled, veined
¼ cup melted butter
1 garlic clove, minced
¼ cup dry white wine
Salt, pepper

Toss shrimps in butter with garlic and wine to coat well. Broil about 5 minutes, 3 inches from heat. Season with salt and pepper.

SHRIMPS A LA MANN
(4 servings)

This dish was a specialty of the late Gus Mann, Chicago restaurateur. The recipe is my adaptation of his. If you like shrimps, you'll love 'em like this.

1 pound raw jumbo shrimps, peeled
2 tablespoons soft butter
1 tablespoon finely minced parsley
1 sliver garlic, mashed
2 tablespoons dry Sherry
¼ teaspoon worcestershire sauce
1 tablespoon fine dry bread crumbs
About 6 slices bacon, cut in half
1 cup wild rice cooked tender in
3 cups clear chicken broth, well-seasoned

Make a deep cut in each shrimp when you remove the vein down the back, to hold the filling. Cream together the butter, parsley, garlic, wine, worcestershire sauce and bread crumbs. Fill the tunnels in the shrimps. Wrap each shrimp in a half slice of bacon and broil until bacon is crisp. Then bed the shrimp on the wild rice on a heatproof platter and heat 2 or 3 minutes in a hot oven, 450 degrees, to blend the flavors.

Peach or strawberry cup: put a ripe peach half or a huge sweet strawberry in a sherbet glass or Champagne saucer. Pour chilled Champagne over it.

SHRIMPS BORDELAISE
(4 servings)

Here's a wonderful way to break that old rule about always serving white wine with seafood.

1 pound raw shrimps, shelled, veined
1 onion, shredded
1 carrot, shredded
1 tablespoon chopped chives
¼ cup butter
2 tablespoons brandy, optional
1 cup dry red wine
2 tablespoons tomato paste
½ teaspoon salt; pepper
2 tablespoons butter
1 tablespoon chopped parsley

Cook onion, carrot and chives in butter until tender. Add shrimps; cook, shaking pan frequently, for about 10 minutes. Sprinkle brandy over shrimps; touch with a lighted match and let burn for a moment. Add wine, tomato paste and seasonings. Cover and simmer 15 minutes. Place shrimps on heated platter. Cook sauce to half the quantity by boiling for about 10 minutes. Stir in 2 tablespoons butter and pour over shrimps. Sprinkle with chopped parsley.

SHRIMPS WITH WILD RICE

(6 very generous servings)

You'd pay dearly for such a dish in a fine restaurant!

½ pound wild rice, washed, cooked in broth
1 tablespoon butter
1½ pounds shrimps, cooked, shelled, veined
1 clove garlic, minced
½ cup chopped onion
1 green pepper, chopped
½ pound mushrooms, sliced
2 tablespoons butter
½ cup Sauterne or other white table wine
1 can consommé diluted with 1 can water
Salt, pepper
1 tablespoon cornstarch

Cook rice in 3 cups chicken broth or consommé about 25 minutes or until tender, not stirring but lifting with a fork occasionally to prevent sticking. Rice should absorb all liquid and should not have to be drained. When tender add butter to it. Sauté garlic, onion, green pepper and mushrooms in butter until lightly browned; add wine and consommé and simmer gently for several minutes. Add salt and pepper as needed. Mix cornstarch to a paste with a little water and stir into sauce. Cook until thickened, stirring constantly. Place prepared shrimps on a bed of the wild rice in a casserole, pour sauce over them and bake 15 minutes at 375 degrees.

SPECIAL SHRIMP CURRY
(4 to 5 servings)

Use your chafing dish for this specialty.

⅓ cup butter
1 medium onion, minced
2 stalks celery, minced
1 carrot, scraped and grated
1 tart apple, peeled, cored and grated
2 tablespoons chopped parsley
1 tablespoon curry powder
½ cup flour
3 cups chicken stock or bouillon
½ cup cream or evaporated milk
3 tablespoons Sherry
1 teaspoon monosodium glutamate
Salt to taste

1½ pounds cooked shrimps, peeled and cleaned

Melt butter in top of large double boiler over direct heat; add onion, celery, carrot, apple and parsley; sauté gently 5 minutes. Blend in curry powder and flour; add chicken stock and cream; cook slowly, stirring constantly, until mixture boils and thickens. Add Sherry, monosodium glutamate, salt and shrimps. Place over hot water, cover and cook 20 to 30 minutes before serving on rice with chutney, chopped cashews and any other curry condiments you may want.

TROUT WITH ANCHOVIES
(6 servings)

A Chablis would be delicious with these trout, even though they're prepared with Sherry.

- 6 cleaned trout
- Salt, pepper, flour
- 6 tablespoons butter or oil
- 1 can (2 oz.) anchovy fillets, diced
- 1 cup dry Sherry
- Juice of 1 lemon
- 2 tablespoons chopped parsley
- ½ teaspoon dried mint leaves

Season trout with salt and pepper, roll in flour and cook in 4 tablespoons of the butter or oil for about 10 minutes or until browned. Cook diced anchovy fillets in remaining butter or oil for 3 or 4 minutes; add Sherry, lemon juice, chopped parsley and mint. Simmer sauce a minute or two. Place trout on hot platter and pour sauce over fish.

• • • • • • • • • • • • • • • • • • • •

BRAZILIAN STUFFED WHITEFISH
(6 servings)

Talk about epicurean fare—this is it!

- 3-pound whitefish or trout
- 2 tablespoons butter
- 1 onion, chopped
- 1 teaspoon salt
- ¼ teaspoon pepper
- 1 tablespoon minced parsley
- 1 bay leaf
- ¾ pound cooked shrimps
- ¾ cup bread crumbs

Trout with Anchovies

• • • • • • • • • • • • • • • • • • • •

1 cup white table wine
1 pint oysters

Have your fish dealer clean and scale the fish, leaving head and tail intact. Wash in cold water and dry. For stuffing, melt butter in a skillet, add onion, salt, pepper, parsley and bay leaf. Cook until onion is lightly browned. Sauté shrimps a minute in the same skillet, then add crumbs and liquid from oysters. Stuff fish rather loosely and close cavity by inserting skewers at intervals and lacing with string. Place in shallow baking pan with wine. Brush well with butter and bake at 400 degrees for 45 minutes, basting with the wine occasionally, if you like. Add oysters to pan last 5 minutes. They are a garnish.

MEATS

GREEN PEPPER STEAK

(4 servings)

White wine may be used in place of red wine, without impairing this good dish.

- 1½ pounds round steak
- Flour, salt, pepper
- ¼ cup oil
- 3 green peppers, cut in strips
- 2 onions chopped
- 1 cup stock or broth
- ½ cup red table wine
- 1 teaspoon worcestershire sauce

Cut the steak into serving-size pieces, flour and season, and brown on both sides in hot oil. Prepare vegetables, setting green peppers aside, and adding onions to meat, along with 1 cup stock. Cover and simmer gently until meat is tender, 1 hour. Add peppers, wine and worcestershire. Cover and cook gently 20 minutes longer. Remove meat and vegetables to hot platter and thicken drippings for gravy, if necessary.

BOEUF BOURGUIGNON
(10 servings)

Basically simple, this classic French dish is deservedly famous.

- 5 pounds boneless beef, cut in large cubes
- 1½ pounds (about 10 medium) onions, diced
- 2 carrots, diced
- ⅓ cup butter
- 6 slices bacon, cut crosswise in strips
- ½ cup flour
- 2 tablespoons brandy
- 1½ to 2 cups red table wine
- Parsley, thyme, bay leaves
- Salt, pepper
- 1 pound mushrooms, sliced and browned in ¼ cup butter

Brown onions and carrots in butter; remove from pan and add beef and bacon. Brown meats. Stir in flour. Pour brandy over meat and set aflame. Add vegetables, wine, herbs, salt and pepper and cover. Simmer 45 minutes. Remove meat from sauce; put sauce through strainer or food mill and return to pan with meat. Add mushrooms and simmer for 2 hours, covered. Serve with croutons.

Baste a beef roast with Burgundy or Claret, a lamb or veal roast with Sauterne.

Marinate lamb in Rosé wine with sliced lemon, sliced onion, rosemary and peppercorns. Use the marinade to baste while roasting.

BEEF IN HERB WINE SAUCE
(4 to 6 servings)

Serve this gourmet entree over fluffy rice and with a green salad.

- 2 pounds lean sirloin tip, cut into 1½-inch cubes
- 3 or 4 medium onions, sliced
- 2 tablespoons oil
- 1½ tablespoons flour
- 1 cup beef bouillon
- 1½ cups red table wine
- ¼ teaspoon each marjoram, thyme, oregano
- 1 teaspoon salt
- ½ teaspoon pepper
- ½ pound fresh mushrooms, sliced lengthwise, sautéed in ¼ cup butter

Sauté onions in oil until yellow; remove from pan, add meat cubes, sprinkle lightly with flour, and brown meat. Add half the bouillon, half the wine and the herbs and seasonings. Cover pan tightly and simmer over low heat (or in a 300 degree oven) about 2 hours, gradually adding remaining bouillon and wine. Add onions and mushrooms, cook about 30 minutes longer or until meat is tender.

• • • • • • • • • • • • • • • • • • • •

HAMBURGERS JEREZ
(4 big ones)

Outdoor appetites are kindled by the smell of these marinated burgers cooking.

- 1 pound ground beef chuck
- 1 teaspoon salt
- ¼ teaspoon pepper

BURGUNDY POT ROAST

(8 or more servings)

This unusually delicious beef makes wonderful hot or cold sandwiches later in the week.

5 pounds beef rump or chuck, rolled and tied
Flour, salt, pepper
2 tablespoons drippings or oil
1 8-oz. can tomato sauce
1 cup Burgundy
½ cup each, finely chopped onion and celery
¼ cup finely chopped parsley
¼ teaspoon each, oregano and sweet basil

Dredge meat with flour seasoned with salt and pepper. Brown slowly on all sides in drippings. Add all remaining ingredients; season to taste with salt and pepper. Cover and simmer gently about 4 hours, or until beef is tender, turning meat occasionally. Transfer to hot platter. Measure liquid in kettle and add water if necessary to make 4 cups; heat to boiling. Blend ¼ cup flour with ½ cup cold water to make a smooth paste; stir slowly into boiling liquid; cook, stirring constantly, for 2 to 3 minutes. Taste and add salt and pepper, if necessary. Serve with meat.

• • • • • • • • • • • • • • • • • • • •

½ cup soy sauce
½ cup Sherry
½ teaspoon ginger
4 split, toasted buns

Mix meat, salt and pepper and shape into four patties. Marinate for an hour in mixture of soy sauce, Sherry and ginger. Drain and cook burgers on grill of outdoor fire or broil them.

CASTILIAN VEAL

(6 to 8 servings)

Olives and Sherry keep this a Spanish dish.

- 1 small leg of veal, about 4 pounds
- 3 strips bacon
- 1 carrot, cut in slivers
- ½ cup olive oil (or salad oil)
- 1 tablespoon flour
- ¼ cup Sherry
- 2 tablespoons water
- 12 small white onions, peeled
- ½ cup green olives, pitted, or stuffed olives
- 1 bay leaf
- ⅛ teaspoon thyme

Insert strips of bacon and slivers of carrot in slits in veal. Salt and pepper the meat. Brown in oil in roasting pan. Stir in flour, add Sherry and water. Cover and cook until tender, at 325 degrees about 2 to 2½ hours. After the first hour add onions, olives, bay leaf and thyme. When ready to serve, slice meat, arrange on a hot platter and garnish with onions and olives.

• • • • • • • • • • • • • • • • • • • •

VEAL SCALLOPINE ALLA MARSALA

(4 servings)

An Italian favorite, the dish is easy to prepare.

- 4 flattened slices veal cutlet
- Grated parmesan cheese
- ¼ cup butter
- Salt, pepper

STUFFED VEAL CHOPS CHABLIS
(4 servings)

If you have Virginia ham to use in the filling, the chops are special!

4 veal chops, about 1¼ inches thick
1½ cups soft bread crumbs
½ cup ground or minced cooked ham
1 tablespoon minced onion
3 tablespoons melted butter
Salt, pepper, flour
3 tablespoons bacon drippings or other fat
1 cup Chablis, Sauterne or other white table wine
1 can condensed cream of mushroom soup

Have each chop slit from fat side to bone to form a pocket. Mix bread crumbs, ham, onion and butter; season with salt and pepper; stuff chops with the mixture. Skewer openings. Dredge chops with seasoned flour. Brown on both sides in hot drippings; add wine. Cover and simmer gently for 45 minutes or until chops are very tender. Place on heated platter. Measure 1 cup of skillet liquid, combine with mushroom soup, heat to boiling, season to taste with salt and pepper and serve with the chops.

• • • • • • • • • • • • • • • • • • • •

½ cup Marsala
1 teaspoon meat extract or sauce

Dip the cleaver-flattened, thin slices of meat into grated cheese, and sauté in butter until browned on each side. Season with salt and pepper. Transfer to hot platter. Add meat extract and wine to skillet, simmer a few minutes and pour over meat. Serve at once. One cup diced mushrooms may be sautéed in the butter after the meat.

VEAL CHOPS PARMESAN WITH WHITE WINE
(6 servings)

Even without the kidneys, chops fixed like this are epicurean food.

- 6 veal loin chops, kidneys attached, ¾-inch thick
- ⅓ cup fresh lime juice
- Salt, pepper
- ¼ cup melted butter
- Flour
- ¾ cup grated parmesan cheese
- ½ cup butter
- 1¼ cups Chablis or other white table wine

Sprinkle chops on both sides with lime juice, salt and coarse freshly ground pepper. Drip with melted butter, sprinkle flour over them and then sprinkle liberally with grated parmesan cheese, patting the cheese into chops so they are well-coated. Let stand for a few minutes, then turn chops and coat the second side with butter, flour and cheese. (This procedure is best done on a sheet of waxed paper.) Let chops stand for about an hour. Sauté chops quickly in butter until browned on both sides. When turning, use a heavy pancake turner and scrape them from the bottom of skillet so coating does not stick to pan. Pour wine around chops. Cover and simmer 30 to 40 minutes.

Canned consommé with a few spoonfuls of red wine in it is an excellent appetizer.

Veal Chops Parmesan with White Wine

HAM AND SWEET POTATO CASSEROLE
(6 servings)

It's even easier out of cans!

- 6 medium cooked or canned sweet potatoes (yams), cut in halves
- 3 cups diced or sliced ham
- 1 glass currant or other tart jelly
- 3 tablespoons brown sugar
- 2 tablespoons butter
- ¼ cup Sherry
- Fine buttered crumbs

Combine ham and sweet potatoes in buttered baking dish. Mix jelly, sugar, butter and wine and pour over ham and sweets. Top with crumbs and bake at 375 degrees until hot and glazed, about 20 minutes.

• •

*ROAST LEG OF LAMB, LAZIO**
(about 6 servings)

Frascati or Soave might be the wine for this roast.

- 1 leg of lamb, about 7 pounds
- 1 clove garlic, cut in slivers
- ½ teaspoon rosemary leaves

* Region of Rome, Italy.

BARBECUED PORK TENDERLOIN
(4 servings)

Sherry, soy sauce and honey give this unusual barbecue sauce a celestial flavor.

2 pork tenderloins, about 1½ pounds each
2 tablespoons soy sauce
2 tablespoons Sherry
3 tablespoons honey
¼ teaspoon powdered ginger
1 teaspoon salt

Place tenderloins in a large bowl. Combine remaining ingredients and pour over meat. Cover and chill several hours or overnight. Bake in a covered casserole at 350 degrees for 2 hours. Remove cover last 30 minutes. Baste with sauce a few times during baking. Cut into thin slices.

• •

Salt, pepper
Olive oil, butter
1 cup dry white wine or Vermouth

Insert garlic slivers and rosemary leaves into slits cut in lamb. Rub with salt and pepper and sprinkle with olive oil. Dot with butter. Brown quickly in a 450 degree oven, reduce heat to 325 degrees, pour wine over meat and continue to roast until lamb is tender, allowing about 20 minutes per pound.

ROAST LEG OF LAMB, ROSEMARY
(6 servings)

Steamed new potatoes in butter and baby peas will make a memorable dinner of such a roast.

- 6-pound leg of lamb
- Salt and pepper
- ¾ teaspoon rosemary
- 1 carrot, sliced
- 1 stalk celery, chopped
- 2 leeks, sliced
- 2 tablespoons butter
- 2 cups dry Sauterne
- 2 cups water

Place leg of lamb in a roasting pan and sprinkle with salt and pepper and ¼ teaspoon rosemary. Cook carrot, celery and leeks in saucepan with butter for 5 minutes, stirring frequently. Add ½ cup each Sauterne and water. Remove from heat. Pour vegetables and liquid around the lamb. Roast at 325 degrees for 2½ to 3 hours, adding wine and water in equal proportions as necessary. Baste occasionally after the first hour of cooking. When lamb is cooked, remove to a hot platter and keep warm. Skim off fat in roaster and add 1 cup each Sauterne and water and ½ teaspoon rosemary. Season with salt and pepper. Thicken, if you wish, with a flour paste. Strain gravy and serve with roast.

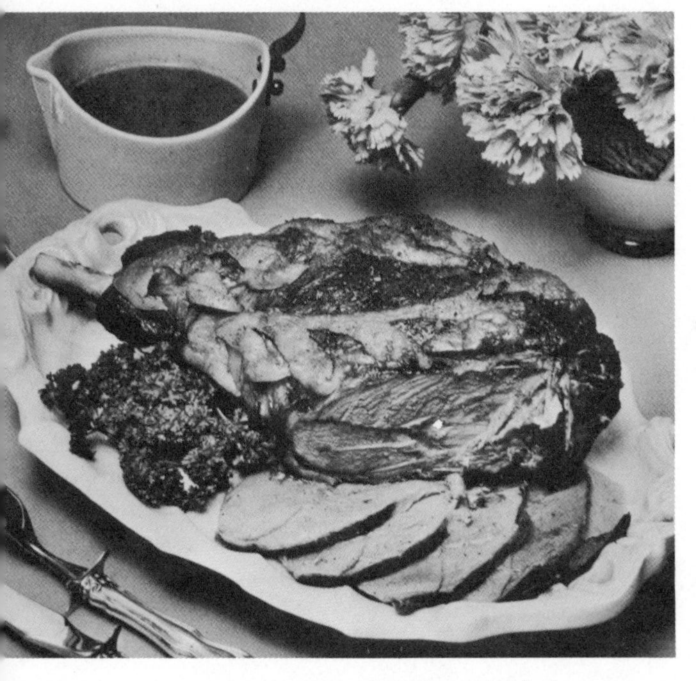

Roast Leg of Lamb, Rosemary

SPICY VENISON ROAST
(8 to 10 servings)

A rump roast of beef may be cooked this way, too.

- 1 (5 pound) venison roast
- 1 cup Burgundy
- 2 tablespoons wine vinegar
- ⅓ cup broth or water
- ½ teaspoon dried dill
- ½ teaspoon seasoned salt
- ⅛ teaspoon garlic powder
- ⅓ cup chili sauce
- 1 tablespoon instant minced onion

Trim meat removing any dry pieces, skin and fat; wipe with a damp cloth. Combine wine, wine vinegar, broth (or water), dill, salt and garlic powder. Pour over meat, cover and marinate in refrigerator overnight, turning several times. Drain well, saving marinade. Brown meat on all sides in hot drippings or oil. Add chili sauce and onion to drained marinade; pour half over meat. Cover and cook until tender in hot oven, 425 degrees, allowing about 20 minutes to the pound. Baste with remaining marinade during cooking period. Skim and discard any excess fat from pan juices; thicken remaining liquid if you like.

For ham or corned beef: prepared mustard thinned with white wine. Or try something hotter—dry mustard mixed to a paste with wine.

POULTRY

CHICKEN AND HAM IMPERIAL
(6 servings)

This chafing dish specialty is easy to prepare, wonderful to eat.

- ½ cup butter
- ½ cup flour
- 1 quart milk or milk and chicken stock
- ½ pound fresh mushrooms, sliced and sautéed in 3 tablespoons butter
- 3 cups diced cooked chicken and ham, any proportion
- ½ cup Sherry
- 1½ cups grated sharp cheddar cheese
- 2 teaspoons minced onion
- 2 teaspoons salt (taste to be sure)
- ½ teaspoon freshly ground black pepper
- ½ cup slivered toasted almonds (optional)

Melt butter in saucepan or chafing dish, blend in flour; add milk and stir to smooth sauce. Add mushrooms and chicken and ham, wine, cheese, onion and seasonings. Stir thoroughly and heat until bubbly. Sprinkle with almonds if you use them. Serve on toast points or hot rice.

CHICKEN BAKED IN FOIL
(4 servings)

This isn't a bad idea for camping out; cooking can be done on a grill.

- 2½ to 3 pound chicken, quartered
- Oil for browning
- 12 mushrooms
- 12 small white onions
- 1 teaspoon salt
- ½ teaspoon pepper
- ½ teaspoon paprika
- 1 teaspoon chopped parsley
- ½ cup white table wine

Brown chicken quarters lightly in oil. Sauté onions and mushrooms. Tear from a roll of aluminum foil 12 inches wide, 4 pieces, each 14 inches long. Butter center of each. Set a quarter of chicken, 3 onions and 3 mushroom caps on each; then season with the salt, pepper, paprika and parsley. Pour 2 tablespoons wine over each portion. Bring edges of foil up over chicken and double fold to make it tight. Set packets on a cooky sheet and bake an hour at 425 degrees. (You need a hotter than usual oven because of the foil insulation.) Turn oven down to 300 degrees to hold chicken until you are ready to serve it. It waits nicely for guests.

Try Vermouth for a chicken marinade or basting sauce. You'll have everybody guessing.

ARROZ CON POLLO
(8 or more servings)

Here's Sherried, saffroned perfection from Latin America.

- 2 chickens, about 3 pounds each, or 16 pieces chicken
- Flour, salt, pepper for coating
- 6 shallots or green onions, sliced
- 2 medium onions, sliced thin
- 1 clove garlic, minced
- ½ cup hot oil
- 6 fresh tomatoes, peeled
- 2 green peppers, diced
- 2 cups chicken broth (from necks, backs, giblets)
- 1 rounded teaspoon saffron
- 2 teaspoons salt (taste to be sure)
- 1 pound uncooked rice (2 cups)
- ½ cup Sherry

Sauté onions and garlic in oil in a large skillet, remove from pan and brown chicken pieces (I use just legs, breasts, wings, 16 pieces) after coating with seasoned flour. Return onions to skillet and slice in tomatoes and peppers. Add broth and saffron. Cover and simmer until nearly tender, about an hour. Then add the rice and cook 30 minutes or so longer, until rice is tender and has absorbed moisture. Mixture should be rather dry. Finish with Sherry.

Moisten stuffings with equal parts broth and table wine.

HAWAIIAN CHICKEN FOR A PARTY
(12 servings)

This casserole can be fixed a day early; it always makes a hit.

2 stewing chickens, about 4½ pounds each
1 small fresh coconut
1 fresh pineapple
½ cup butter
½ cup flour
3½ cups coconut water and chicken stock
½ cup Sherry
2 tablespoons chopped preserved ginger
1 cup chopped macadamia nuts, cashews or toasted slivered almonds

Simmer the cut-up chickens in water to cover, with 1½ tablespoons salt, juice of 1 lemon, a cluster of celery tops, a few peppercorns and a bay leaf. Cool in stock, remove meat from bones and dice or slice. Strain stock; chill and remove fat. Bore holes in two eyes of the coconut, drain water and combine with stock to make 3½ cups of liquid. Grate coconut meat. Slice, pare and core pineapple and cut slices in small pieces. (I like to quarter the slices, then slice the quartered pieces very thin.) Melt butter, blend in flour and gradually add stock and coconut water, stirring until thickened. Add Sherry and ginger, and more salt and pepper if needed. Arrange alternate layers of chicken, grated coconut, pineapple, nuts and sauce in baking dish. Bake half an hour at 375 degrees. Cheese or buttered crumbs may be used as a topping, but that's just lily-gilding.

PERUVIAN CHICKEN
(4 to 6 servings)

Guests will beg for this recipe!

- 1 chicken, about 3 pounds, cut up, or 8 to 12 pieces of chicken
- 3 tablespoons butter
- 1 small onion, minced
- 6 whole cloves (or ⅛ teaspoon ground)
- 1 bay leaf
- ½ teaspoon cumin seasoning, or ¼ teaspoon cumin seed
- 1 cup concentrated stock (or canned consommé)
- 1 cup white Port
- ½ cup raisins
- ½ cup shredded blanched almonds
- ½ cup heavy cream
- 2 egg yolks
- ¼ cup more wine
- Salt, pepper

Brown chicken in butter; add onion last few minutes. Add cloves, bay leaf, cumin, stock. Cover and simmer gently. Add Port, raisins, almonds when about half-cooked. Simmer until tender, then mix cream, egg yolks and wine, stir in a little of the hot sauce and pour into the chicken. Stir until thickened, about a minute. Don't let sauce boil. Add salt and pepper if necessary.

CHICKEN MARENGO
(6 servings)

Napoleon's chef cooked the progenitor of this dish on a battlefield.

2 broiler-fryer chickens, cut up
¼ cup olive oil
Salt, pepper
2 tablespoons flour
½ cup stock or water
1 cup white table wine
Bouquet garni*
1 clove garlic, chopped fine
1 tablespoon tomato paste
½ pound mushrooms, sliced

Brown chicken in the oil and season with salt and pepper. Remove chicken from pan. Stir in flour and add stock and wine. When well-blended, add bouquet garni, garlic, tomato paste and mushrooms. Season with more salt and pepper. Add chicken and coat each piece with sauce. Cover, simmer for half an hour, remove herbs and serve.

* Bouquet garni is commonly used in French cooking. It consists of 3 or 4 sprigs of parsley, a sprig of thyme and a small bay leaf tied together. The thyme should be surrounded by the parsley so that the little leaves will not float into the sauce. You may substitute ¼ teaspoon powdered thyme and 1 teaspoon parsley flakes, but tie these in a cheesecloth bag or strain sauce before serving.

• • • • • • • • • • • • • • • • • • • •

CHICKEN ROSÉ (4 servings)

This is an ever-so-easy gourmet dish.

2 large chicken breasts, split (or 4 small ones, boned)
¼ teaspoon garlic salt
½ teaspoon salt
½ teaspoon paprika
2 tablespoons flour
Oil for browning
¼ teaspoon each, dried basil, rosemary (or ½ teaspoon salad herbs)

CHICKEN CACCIATORA
(4 or 5 servings)

Utterly delicious, yet so simple! Mushrooms sometimes are added.

1 chicken, 2½ to 3½ pounds, in pieces
½ cup olive oil
1 sliced onion
1 minced clove garlic
1 can (1 pound 12 oz.) Italian pear tomatoes
1½ teaspoons salt
¼ teaspoon pepper
½ cup red or white table wine (Chianti, perhaps, for this Italian dish)
Chopped parsley

Brown the chicken pieces in the oil, reduce heat, add onion and garlic and sauté until onion is yellow. Drain excess oil. Add tomatoes, seasonings; simmer until chicken is tender and tomatoes are reduced to a thick sauce, about 45 minutes. Taste and add more seasonings if you need them. Add wine the last 15 minutes. Sprinkle with parsley when you've turned the chicken onto a hot platter. *For a special party,* add ¼ pound finely diced ham and ½ pound sliced fresh mushrooms. Sauté both with chicken and seasoning. Mushrooms alone may be added.

• • • • • • • • • • • • • • • • • • • •

½ cup Rosé wine   ½ cup sour cream

Coat chicken with mixture of garlic salt, salt, paprika and flour. Brown in ½ inch oil on all sides. Pour off excess oil, then add herbs and wine. Cover and cook slowly until chicken is tender, about 30 minutes or more. Remove chicken to warm platter. Stir sour cream into drippings and pour sauce around chicken.

CHICKEN LIVER PATÉ
(About 1½ cups)

This is my favorite canape spread.

½ pound chicken livers or calf liver
¼ pound melted butter
1 teaspoon salt
¼ pound fresh mushrooms
¼ cup red table wine or Vermouth
1 slice onion
Freshly ground pepper

Sauté the livers in part of the butter until tender. Add the onion then, too, if you wish. Then put everything into the electric blender and whirl it to a smooth paste. Mushrooms are washed, but not cooked. Chill the mixture and serve for a party with melba toast, crackers or rye bread. I usually double this recipe, line fancy molds with clear gelatin, fill them with the paté and freeze or chill until I need them. Unmolded, with the gelatin coating, the paté is very attractive.

• • • • • • • • • • • • • • • • • • • •

CHICKEN LIVERS EN BROCHETTE
(4 servings)

These are so easy, so good!

1 dozen chicken livers
1 dozen caps from large mushrooms
¼ cup melted butter or margarine
Sherry or Burgundy

CHICKEN LIVERS SAUTÉ, ON TOAST
(4 servings)

Ready in 10 minutes!

- 1 pound fresh or frozen chicken livers
- 3 tablespoons butter
- 1 teaspoon salt
- Pepper
- ¼ teaspoon mixed dried herbs, or a pinch of nutmeg
- ½ cup white or red table wine
- 4 slices trimmed toast, cut in triangles

Cook livers very gently in the butter just until there's no red left in them. Season with salt, pepper and herbs or nutmeg. Place them on toast on serving plates. Add the wine to the skillet or pan, let it simmer a minute or two to loosen all the good little bits of liver, then pour over livers and toast. Good on rice or noodles, too, or as filling for an omelet.

• • • • • • • • • • • • • • • • • • •

- Finely chopped parsley
- Salt, pepper

Wash livers and drain dry. Cut in half and thread onto skewers (small ones) alternately with mushroom caps. Brush with the melted butter and sprinkle with the wine and parsley. Broil until tender, turning several times. This takes only about 15 minutes. As soon as they are heated through, both livers and mushrooms have cooked sufficiently. Sprinkle with salt and coarse pepper and serve.

COQ AU VIN ROUGF
(4 servings)

A French classic, this is an extravagant dish, but perfectly delectable!

- 1 broiler-fryer, quartered
- Salt, pepper, paprika, nutmeg and flour
- ¼ pound salt pork or bacon, cut in strips
- 1 dozen small white onions, peeled
- 2 tablespoons brandy
- 2 cups Burgundy
- 1 teaspoon sugar
- 1 minced clove garlic
- 1 celery top, tied with 5 or 6 sprigs parsley and 1 bay leaf
- Pinch rosemary, pinch thyme
- Cornstarch for thickening
- 8 medium or 4 huge mushrooms, whole, sautéed

Wipe chicken pieces with damp cloth and rub with salt, pepper, paprika and nutmeg. Roll in flour. Cook salt pork or bacon, brown onions gently in the fat, remove from skillet and brown chicken well. Pour brandy over chicken and ignite. When flames die down, add wine, sugar, garlic and herbs, tied together. Return onions to pan. Cover, and bake at 325 degrees until chicken is tender, about 45 minutes. Remove herbs. Thicken sauce with paste of cornstarch and wine or water. The chicken takes on pinkness from the wine. Present chicken in sauce, garnished with the mushrooms.

BAKED TURKEY SANDWICHES
(4 portions)

After a holiday meal of roast turkey, you'll have the makings for many kinds of sandwiches, none more savory than these.

- ¼ cup butter
- ¼ cup flour
- 1⅔ cups milk
- ⅓ cup Sherry
- 1 can (4 oz.) mushroom stems and pieces, drained
- Dash of mace
- Salt and pepper
- 8 slices crisp toast, crusts removed
- 4 servings sliced, cooked turkey
- 8 slices crisp cooked bacon
- ½ cup grated cheddar cheese
- Paprika

Melt butter and stir in flour; add milk and cook, stirring constantly, until mixture boils and thickens. Add wine, mushrooms, mace, salt and pepper. Place 2 slices toast side by side in each of 4 shallow, oval, individual baking dishes. Spread toast with some of the mushroom sauce; top with sliced turkey, then with bacon strips. Pour remaining sauce over all; sprinkle with grated cheese and paprika. Bake 10 minutes or until bubbly at 450 degrees. *Variation:* Place a slice of ham under each portion of turkey, and omit bacon.

SHERRIED TURKEY WITH GRAPES
(4 servings)

It takes but a few minutes to put together this gourmet special.

- 2 cups medium cream sauce*
- ¼ cup Sherry
- ¼ pound mushrooms, sliced lengthwise and sautéed in 2 tablespoons butter
- 2 cups diced cooked turkey (cut in large pieces)
- ½ cup green grapes, halved and seeded
- ½ cup red grapes, halved and seeded

(*Forgotten how to make cream sauce? Melt 4 tablespoons butter, add 4 tablespoons flour, ½ teaspoon salt and a little pepper. Stir well and add gradually 2 cups milk. Stir until smooth and thickened.)

Add wine to cream sauce. Add mushrooms and turkey and heat. Just before serving add grapes. Serve on reheated turkey stuffing, if you have some, or on rice, or in puff-pastry shells. Pineapple may be used instead of grapes. One could add a sprinkling of toasted salted almonds at serving time. Canned, broiled-in-butter mushrooms may be used instead of fresh ones.

For dessert: fresh strawberries chilled in ruby or white Port.

TURKEY TIMBALES WITH MUSHROOM WINE SAUCE
(6 servings)

Who said *leftovers?* You'd never believe it!

- 6 tablespoons butter or margarine
- 6 tablespoons flour
- 1½ cups rich milk
- 1 cup turkey stock or chicken broth
- ½ cup Rhine wine or any white table wine
- 2 cups ground cooked turkey
- 1½ cups soft bread crumbs
- 2 eggs, slightly beaten
- Salt and pepper to taste
- 2 tablespoons minced parsley
- 2-oz. can mushroom pieces

Melt butter and stir in flour; add milk, stock and wine; cook, stirring constantly, until mixture is thickened and smooth. To 1 cup of this sauce add the turkey, bread crumbs, eggs, salt and pepper; blend well, spoon mixture into 6 well-greased custard cups, place in a shallow pan of hot water and bake in a moderate oven, 350 degrees, for 30 minutes or until firm. Add parsley and mushrooms (including the liquid) to remaining sauce; season to taste with salt and pepper; heat over boiling water. Unmold baked timbales and serve with the mushroom sauce.

DUCKLINGS WITH ORANGES
(6 to 8 servings)

A dish such as this is a culinary masterpiece!

2 ducklings, about 5 pounds each
¾ cup butter
½ cup brandy
6 mushrooms, finely chopped
4 orange rinds, finely shredded (outer peel only)
2 teaspoons salt
¼ teaspoon pepper
2 teaspoons tomato paste
2 tablespoons cornstarch
¼ cup water
2 cups stock
1 cup orange juice
1 cup red table wine
2 tablespoons currant jelly
2 bay leaves
½ pound chicken livers
4 tablespoons butter
4 oranges, sectioned (membrane removed)

Have butcher cut each duckling into 8 pieces. Brown pieces quickly in ¾ cup hot butter. Remove excess fat, pour brandy over duck and ignite. When flames have died out, remove duck from pan. Add mushrooms, orange rinds, salt and pepper to liquid remaining in pan and cook over low heat for 5 minutes. Remove from heat and add tomato paste, cornstarch mixed with water, and stock, stirring until smooth. Cook mixture to boiling, and add orange juice, wine and jelly. Return duck to pan, top with bay leaves, cover and cook over low heat for 1 hour. While the duck is cooking, cook chicken livers in butter for 3 or

Ducklings with Oranges

4 minutes. When duck is ready, arrange on warm serving platter, thicken gravy if desired and add chicken livers and orange sections. Heat through, pour over duck and serve.

DUCK WITH MARSALA
(4 servings)

Sicily's dark wine beautifully flavors a sauce for the rich meat of duck.

4 to 5 pound duck, quartered
½ cup flour seasoned with salt, pepper
2 tablespoons butter
½ cup chopped onion
½ green pepper, chopped
½ pound fresh mushrooms, sliced
1 teaspoon grated orange rind
1 cup veal or chicken stock, or bouillon
2 tablespoons tomato paste
½ cup Marsala
Salt and pepper

Coat duck quarters with well-seasoned flour. Add onion, green pepper and mushrooms to butter in skillet and cook until lightly browned. Remove from pan. Add a little more butter to pan and brown duck on all sides. Pour off all fat in pan, return vegetables, add orange rind and stock, cover and simmer gently on top of range or bake in 350 degree over for half an hour. Then add tomato paste and wine, plus salt and pepper if needed. Cover again and cook about an hour longer, until duck is very tender and sauce thickish. Skim excess fat from sauce and serve around duck.

ROAST DUCK WITH WINE SAUCE
(4 servings)

The flavors of duck and red wine—*tres harmonieux!*

4 to 5 pound duck, quartered
2 cups Claret or Burgundy
⅓ cup brandy
½ cup chopped onions
2 tablespoons minced parsley
¾ teaspoon salt
¼ teaspoon pepper
½ pound sliced mushrooms
2 tablespoons flour
¼ cup cold water
Salt, pepper

Arrange duck pieces on rack in open roasting pan. Brown in a 400 degree oven for 30 minutes, then pour off all except ¼ cup of the drippings. Remove rack from pan; place duck in bottom of pan. Mix wine, brandy, onions, parsley, salt, pepper and sliced mushrooms. Pour over duck. Return to oven; reduce heat to 325 degrees. Bake about 1½ hours, or until duck is tender. Baste frequently with sauce. Remove duck from pan and keep warm while preparing gravy. Blend the flour in cold water until smooth. Add to liquid in pan; cook, stirring constantly, until thickened. Add salt and pepper to taste. Place duck on hot platter; cover with thickened sauce.

DESSERTS

BAKED BANANAS HAWAIIAN

(4 servings)

Straight from Honolulu comes this dish, good with meats as well as for dessert.

4 bananas, peeled
½ cup brown sugar, firmly packed
¼ cup pineapple or orange juice
3 tablespoons Sherry, Madeira or Muscatel
½ cup chopped macadamia nuts (blanched almonds will do)
2 tablespoons butter
Nutmeg

Place bananas in small baking dish. Mix sugar, juice and Sherry, and pour over them. Sprinkle with nuts sautéed in butter and with nutmeg. Bake at 350 degrees for about 15 minutes, or until glazed.

"*BIEN ME SABE*"
(6 servings)

Rich, sweet and winey, this Spanish pudding is related to the English trifle.

1 fresh coconut
1 cup sugar
2 sticks cinnamon
8 egg yolks, beaten
½ cup sweet Sherry, Port or Tokay
⅛ teaspoon cinnamon
Sponge cake, pound cake, lemon or white layers (¼ pound)

Drain water from coconut and save. Remove coconut meat from shell and grate (in your electric blender, to make it easy). Combine with coconut water, work with hands to extract the milk, then strain through a cloth, squeezing to get out all the milk. Combine coconut milk with sugar and stick cinnamon, bring to a boil and cook 5 minutes. Carefully stir in beaten egg yolks and cook until thickened, stirring constantly. Remove cinnamon sticks and chill. Cut cake in oblongs to fit bottom of a loaf pan. Pour wine over cake, then the chilled custard. Sprinkle with cinnamon and chill thoroughly. Serve with unsweetened whipped cream. This is a perfect way to use left-over cake.

Baptize each hot baked apple with a tablespoon of Port.

EGGNOG REFRIGERATOR CAKE
(8 servings)

A pretty party dessert that is rich but not too sweet. You might add color by garnishing with maraschino cherries.

- 1 tablespoon (envelope) plain gelatin
- ¼ cup cold water
- 4 eggs, separated
- ½ cup Sherry or Port
- ¼ cup sugar
- 1 cup cream, whipped
- 1 teaspoon vanilla
- 10 ladyfingers, split
- 12 almond macaroons, crumbled

Soften gelatin in cold water; dissolve over boiling water. Beat egg yolks until light; add Sherry gradually, beating constantly. Add gelatin mixture and blend. Beat egg whites until stiff; add sugar gradually, beating after each addition. Fold into yolk mixture. Fold in whipped cream and vanilla. Line loaf pan with split ladyfingers. Alternate layers of eggnog mixture with macaroon crumbs in pan. Chill at least 12 hours. Unmold and spread top and sides with additional whipped cream.

• •

FRUIT MEDLEY WITH PORT
(serves 6)

Try this recipe with fruit variations, such as Royal Ann cherries or canned figs in place of apricots.

- 6 canned pear halves
- 6 canned peach halves
- 6 canned whole apricots
- 1½ cups sugar
- ¾ cup syrup from canned fruit

GLAZED STRAWBERRY PIE
(9 inch pie; 6 cuts)

This is one of my favorites—a beauty!

- 1 quart ripe strawberries
- ¾ cup sugar
- ½ cup water
- ½ cup Port
- 2½ tablespoons cornstarch
- ¼ cup sugar
- ⅛ teaspoon salt
- Baked pastry shell

Wash and stem strawberries and reserve 1 cup of the poorest for the glaze. Cook this cup of berries with the ¾ cup sugar and the water and Port for 5 minutes. Put through a sieve. Add cornstarch with the ¼ cup sugar and the salt. Cook until thick, and cool. Fill shell with rest of berries, whole or halved. Pour glaze over pie and chill before serving. The pie is both beautiful and delicious and doesn't need further glamorizing, but of course you may add whipped cream.

• • • • • • • • • • • • • • • • • • • •

- ¾ cup Port
- 1½ teaspoons grated orange rind
- 1½ teaspoons grated lemon rind
- 1 tablespoon lemon juice

Drain fruit. Arrange 1 pear half, 1 peach half and 1 apricot in each of 6 dessert dishes. Combine remaining ingredients in a saucepan; bring to a boil, stirring until sugar is dissolved; simmer 15 minutes; let cool. Pour cooled syrup over fruit and chill in the refrigerator for several hours before serving.

HOT FRUIT COMPOTE
(8 servings)

Almost any combination of fruit you can think of makes delicious dessert this way.

- 1 can (1 pound 13 oz.) each, pineapple slices, peach halves, pear halves and light sweet cherries
- 2 oranges, sectioned
- 1 cup fresh seedless grapes or halved seeded green grapes
- ⅔ cup brown sugar
- ¼ cup butter
- 1 package (7 oz.) coconut macaroons, crumbled
- ½ cup toasted and slivered almonds
- 1½ cups cream Sherry or other dessert wine

Drain the canned fruits; arrange the fruits in layers in a casserole, sprinkling each layer with brown sugar, dotting with butter and then adding a layer of macaroon crumbs. Wind up with a sprinkling of toasted slivered almonds on top, and add Sherry. Place fruit in a 375 degree oven, turn off heat and leave while you eat the first course.

• • • • • • • • • • • • • • • • • • • •

HASTY LAZY DAISY CAKE
(9 pieces or more)

Serve this cake warm—it's *so* good!

- 1 package white or yellow cake mix
- 3 tablespoons butter
- 6 tablespoons brown sugar
- 2 tablespoons cream

Hot Fruit Compote

• • • • • • • • • • • • • • • • • • • •

2 tablespoons Muscatel
½ cup shredded coconut
¼ cup chopped nuts

Mix the cake as the package directs and bake it in a 9 by 9 by 2 inch pan. Mix butter, sugar, cream, wine, coconut and nuts. When the cake comes out of the oven, spread with the mixture and place cake under broiling unit just long enough to lightly brown and bubble the topping.

PORT WINE CAKE
(9 by 9 by 2 inch cake)

Frost with a lemon butter icing—an unusual teatime treat.

½ cup butter
1 cup sugar
2 teaspoons baking powder
⅛ teaspoon salt
1¾ cups sifted cake flour
½ cup Port
Grated rind of 1 lemon
4 egg whites, beaten stiff

Cream butter and sugar well. Sift baking powder, salt and cake flour. Add alternately with wine to creamed mixture. Add lemon rind. Beat egg whites until stiff and fold them into the batter. Bake cake in an oiled, floured pan at 350 degrees for about 45 minutes.

• • • • • • • • • • • • • • • • • • • •

SHERRY WINE CHIFFON PIE
(9 inch pie; 6 cuts)

This is an old recipe and one of the best of its kind.

1 cup milk
½ cup sugar
3 eggs, separated
⅛ teaspoon nutmeg
¼ teaspoon salt
1½ tablespoons unflavored gelatin
4 tablespoons milk
1 cup Sherry
1 cup heavy cream, whipped

JELLIED CHERRIES OR PEACHES IN PORT
(6 servings)

Two to four times this recipe makes an exciting buffet mold.

½ cup Port
1 cup sliced fresh pitted dark sweet cherries, or sliced fresh or canned peaches
1 package strawberry-flavored gelatin
1½ cups hot water

Pour wine over fruit and let stand while preparing gelatin. Dissolve gelatin in hot water. Cool and add fruit and wine. Chill until slightly thickened, then turn into large mold or individual molds and chill until firm. Serve plain or with chilled soft custard, sour cream or whipped cream. *Variants:* Pears may be used in the same recipe. Seedless grapes, Port and orange-flavored gelatin are another good combination.

• • • • • • • • • • • • • • • • • • •

¼ teaspoon vanilla
Baked pastry shell or graham cracker crust

Combine milk and sugar and bring to scalding. Stir a little of the hot milk mixture into the beaten yolks, add nutmeg and salt, return to hot mixture and cook over low heat, stirring until mixture coats a spoon. Remove from heat and add the gelatin which has been softened in the 4 table-spoons milk. Stir to dissolve. Stir in wine gradually. Chill until mixture begins to thicken. Fold in stiff beaten egg whites, then fold in half the whipped cream. Turn into pie shell and chill until firm. Top with remaining whipped cream flavored with vanilla. Slivered toasted almonds could be sprinkled over the whipped cream.

WINE DATE CAKE SQUARES
(9 by 12 pan; about 24 pieces)

Serve these spicy, winey, delicious cakes at teatime, or drop a spoonful of whipped cream on each and serve as dessert. For Christmas cooky collections, cut 48 tiny squares.

¼ cup shortening
1 cup brown sugar, firmly packed
1 egg
1½ cups sifted flour
1 teaspoon soda
¼ teaspoon salt
1 teaspoon cinnamon
1 teaspoon nutmeg
1 package (8 oz.) pitted dates, cut up
1 cup coarsely cut walnuts or pecans
1 cup Muscatel, Port or Sherry

Cream shortening and sugar well; add unbeaten egg and beat until blended. Mix and sift flour, soda, salt and spices. Add dates and nuts. Alternately add flour mixture and wine, beating well. Turn into greased, floured pan. Bake 30 minutes at 350 degrees. Cool slightly before cutting. Sprinkle with powdered sugar, if you like.

STRAWBERRY MACAROON WHIP
(6 portions)

Nothing to it, but how delicious a dessert this is!

1 pint strawberries, sliced and lightly sugared
3 tablespoons Port or Muscatel
2 cups coarse macaroon crumbs
1 cup heavy cream, whipped

Sprinkle wine on macaroon crumbs and let stand half an hour. Fold berries, crumbs and cream together and pile in sherbet dishes.

STRAWBERRY PORTCAKE
(4 servings)

Here's a ruby-sauced version of an old favorite dessert.

- 2 cups fresh strawberries, sliced
- ½ cup red currant or raspberry jelly
- ¼ cup California Port
- ½ teaspoon grated orange rind
- 1½ teaspoons cornstarch
- 2 teaspoons water
- 2 teaspoons lemon juice
- 4 individual biscuit or sponge shortcakes

Combine jelly, Port and orange rind; heat slowly until jelly is melted. Stir cornstarch into water; add to jelly-wine mixture; cook and stir until sauce boils and becomes clear and thickened. Stir in lemon juice; remove from heat. Cool a few minutes, then add berries and spoon warm over split biscuit or sponge shortcakes. You may top each serving with sour cream, whipped cream or vanilla ice cream.

ZABAGLIONE
(4 servings)

One of the simplest, most continental of desserts, this warm whip may be used as a sauce or pudding.

- 3 egg yolks
- 3 tablespoons sugar
- ½ cup Marsala

Beat egg yolks, adding sugar gradually, until thick and light. Add wine and mix well. Pour mixture into a saucepan or chafing dish and heat quickly, whipping constantly until fluffy and thick. Remove from heat at once and pour into small glasses. Eat with a spoon.

MAY WINE BERRY MOLD

(6 servings)

This delicate gelatin mixture can be salad or dessert.

- 1 tablespoon unflavored gelatin
- 1 bottle (7 oz.) sparkling water
- 1 cup May wine
- 3 tablespoons sugar
- 1 pint fresh raspberries or strawberries
- 1 package (3 oz.) cream cheese

Soften gelatin in ¼ cup sparkling water. Dissolve over boiling water. Mix with remaining water and wine. Add sugar. Chill until partially thickened. Fold half of berries into half of gelatin and turn into individual molds. Chill. Beat cheese with electric mixer until smooth. Add remaining gelatin and beat until blended. Pour over first layer, and chill until firm. When ready to serve, unmold and garnish with remaining berries.

WINE-BAKED PEACHES

(6 servings)

Wine, mace and lemon all add up to something exquisite in peaches.

- 6 ripe peaches, peeled
- 1 tablespoon butter
- ½ teaspoon mace
- ½ cup water
- 1 cup sugar
- 1 lemon, juice and grated rind
- ¼ cup white Port

Place peaches in a baking dish which has a cover. Add other ingredients, cover and bake at 375 degrees until fruit is tender, ½ hour or longer. Chill before serving.

ALMOND SHERRY PRALINES
(2 dozen)

A box of these delights is a welcome Christmas or birthday gift.

- 3 cups light brown sugar
- 1 cup milk
- ½ teaspoon grated orange rind
- ½ cup Sherry
- 2 tablespoons butter
- ⅛ teaspoon salt
- 1 cup halves of blanched almonds

Bring sugar and milk to boil in heavy saucepan, stirring until boiling point is reached. Add orange rind and Sherry, stir until mixture again comes to a boil, then cook without stirring to soft ball stage, 240 degrees. Add butter, salt, nuts and cool to lukewarm without stirring. Beat until creamy, then drop from spoon onto waxed paper. Wrap each praline in waxed paper, or better, transparent plastic.

Like cinnamon toast? Mix a little Sherry with your cinnamon, sugar and butter topping and broil until bubbly. So *good!*

SHERRIED FUDGE
(about 36 pieces)

This is a failure-proof, uncooked fudge, and simply delicious.

- 1 package (6 oz.) semi-sweet chocolate pieces
- 2 tablespoons butter
- 1 pound confectioners' sugar, sifted
- ¼ teaspoon salt
- 1 egg yolk, slightly beaten
- ¼ cup Sherry
- ½ teaspoon vanilla
- 1 cup chopped pecans, walnuts, black walnuts or filberts, optional

Heat the chocolate and butter over water, stirring until melted. Add alternate portions of sugar and salt, and egg yolk, Sherry and vanilla. Work until smooth. Add nuts, if you use them. Mix well and either spread evenly in a well-buttered 8-inch pan, then cut into squares, or knead into two rolls, and slice the rolls into pieces.

• •

SHERRIED TUNA PIMIENTO DIP
(about 2 cups)

The dip is a pretty pastel with a flavor everyone tries to analyze.

- 1 (4½ oz.) can pimientos, drained and ground or chopped
- 2 3-oz. packages cream cheese, mashed
- 1 can (6½ to 7 oz.) tuna

HOLIDAY CHEESE BOWL
(about 1¾ cups)

Your guests will ask for this recipe!

- ½ cup Sauterne, Chablis or other white dinner wine
- 1 tablespoon instant minced onion
- ¾ teaspoon powdered sage
- ½ teaspoon dry mustard
- Pinch black pepper
- ½ pound cheddar cheese
- ¼ pound blue cheese
- 2 tablespoons toasted sesame seeds

Combine wine, onion and spices. Let stand about 10 minutes. Crumble cheeses into mixing bowl. Beat in wine mixture until thoroughly blended. Heap into serving bowl and sprinkle with toasted sesame seeds. Spread may be stored, covered, in refrigerator until ready to use, or frozen if long storage is necessary. *Variation:* For a soft cheese dip, add ½ pint (1 cup) sour cream and seasoned salt to taste to above recipe. Makes about 2½ cups dip.

• • • • • • • • • • • • • • • • • • • •

- ¼ cup Sherry
- 2 tablespoons mayonnaise
- 1 teaspoon grated onion
- ½ teaspoon worcestershire sauce
- Salt, pepper, garlic salt

Combine ingredients and whip in your mixer or blender. Heap into a bowl and keep cold until ½ hour before you wish to serve. Accompany with potato chips, crackers or melba toast.

SCRAMBLED EGGS WITH CHABLIS
(4 servings)

6 eggs
¼ cup cream
¼ cup Chablis or any white table wine
½ teaspoon salt
Few grains pepper
2 tablespoons butter
3-oz. package cream cheese, cubed

Beat eggs lightly; add cream, wine, salt and pepper. Melt butter in skillet, chafing dish or double boiler. When hot, pour in the egg mixture. Stir occasionally until eggs are almost firm, still very moist. Stir in the cheese and serve without further cooking.

• • • • • • • • • • • • • • • • • • •

SWITZERLAND DÉLICES
(50 to 60 small croquettes)

These ethereal morsels may be shaped into tiny balls, if you wish. They'll be gone in no time, either way, and guests will cry for more!

3 tablespoons butter
½ cup flour
2½ cups milk
¾ cup white wine
1 teaspoon salt
Pepper to taste
¾ pound grated Swiss cheese
5 egg yolks, beaten
2 eggs for coating
½ cup milk
2 tablespoons oil
Flour
Fine bread crumbs

Switzerland Délices

Melt butter over low heat, add flour and stir until golden colored. Add milk, stir until smooth and cook until thickened (about 10 minutes), stirring constantly. Boil wine to reduce to ½ cup, and add it to sauce. Season with salt and pepper and remove from heat. Add cheese and stir until melted. Add egg yolks last and blend well. Spread in a well-buttered shallow dish, 7 by 11 inches. Cool. Cover with waxed paper and chill for 2 hours or until needed. Cut into rectangles. Beat eggs with milk and oil. Roll each croquette in flour, dip in egg mixture, drain well and cover completely with fine crumbs. Fry in deep fat at 360 degrees until golden brown. Serve immediately.

SWISS CHEESE PIE

(6 servings)

On the order of a quiche Lorraine, this delicacy makes a perfect late supper or light lunch.

PIE CRUST:

1½ cups flour
⅛ teaspoon salt
9 tablespoons butter
1 egg

FILLING:

½ pound aged Swiss cheese, thinly sliced or shredded
2 green onions with about 3 inches of green tops, thinly sliced
3 eggs
1 cup cream
¼ cup Riesling or other white table wine
½ clove garlic, crushed fine
¼ teaspoon freshly ground black pepper
Nutmeg

Sift flour and salt for crust into mixing bowl. With a pastry blender or two knives, cut butter into dry ingredients until particles are fine. Add beaten egg, and toss with fork until thoroughly blended. Press mixture into bottom and sides of 9 inch pie pan. Prick all over with floured fork. Bake at 425 degrees 20 minutes or until golden brown. Cool on rack. *To make filling:* Arrange Swiss cheese over bottom of cooled shell. Sprinkle with onions. Beat together the eggs, cream, wine, garlic and pepper until thoroughly mixed. Pour into shell and sprinkle lightly with nutmeg. Bake at 325 degrees for 50 to 55 minutes or until custard is set and barely tinged with brown. Cut into wedges and serve immediately with chilled white wine (the kind used in the pie) and a salad.

Swiss Cheese Pie

WINE JELLY

(about 5 glasses, 6 oz. each)

A glass of red wine jelly is a welcomed Christmas gift.

3 cups sugar
2 cups wine (any kind!)
½ bottle fruit pectin

Measure sugar and wine into top of double boiler. Place over rapidly boiling water and heat 2 minutes, stirring constantly. Remove from water. Add pectin, stirring constantly until well mixed. Pour quickly into glasses. Paraffin at once. Red and Rosé wines make the prettiest jellies; Sherry, Rhine wine, Chablis and other whites also make distinguished ones. Burgundy jelly is marvelous with game and beef.

WINEY FRENCH BREAD

(1 loaf)

Garlic may be added, if you like. Either way, this is great with spaghetti.

1 long loaf French bread
½ cup soft butter
¼ cup red table wine
½ cup grated parmesan cheese

Cut bread not quite through the loaf in thickish slices. Spread whipped-together mixture of butter, wine and cheese between slices and over bread. Bake at 400 degrees 10 minutes or until hot. A crushed clove of garlic and a sprinkle of mixed salad herbs may be added to the spread.

SHERRIED FRENCH TOAST
(4 to 6 servings)

There are three ways to cook this sophisticated dish.

3 eggs beaten with
½ cup milk,
½ cup Sherry, and
½ teaspoon salt
6 to 10 slices of bread, crusts trimmed if you like, cut in halves if you like

Place egg mixture in shallow dish and dip bread into it, allowing it to soak. Let drain a second or two, then sauté in butter in a heavy skillet, turning when golden brown underneath; or fry in deep fat at 365 degrees until golden; or bake on a buttered cooky sheet at 450 degrees for 8 to 10 minutes, turn and bake 5 minutes longer. Serve with butter and maple syrup, jelly or jam. Wonderful with applesauce. Slices may be dipped in confectioners' sugar after French frying.

CHEDDAR CHEESE SPREAD WITH PORT
(1 cup)

Use the sharpest cheddar you can find. This is good!

¼ cup Port or Sherry
2 tablespoons cream
¼ teaspoon paprika
Dash onion salt
½ pound sharp cheddar cheese, diced

Put everything into your electric blender and mix smooth. The cheese can be molded in a small bowl by chilling it.

SOUTHWESTERN CHILI BEANS

(6 or more servings)

Almost any kind of beans will be good cooked this way.

- 1 pound pink or red beans
- Cold water
- 1 quart boiling water
- 2 onions, chopped
- 1 clove garlic, chopped
- 6 slices bacon, finely cut
- 1 cup Zinfandel or other red table wine
- 1 can (8 oz.) tomato sauce
- 2 tablespoons chili powder
- ½ teaspoon cumin seed
- 2 teaspoons salt

Wash beans; soak overnight in cold water. Drain. Put in heavy kettle with boiling water and remaining ingredients. Cover; simmer gently until beans are tender and sauce is thick and rich, 3 to 4 hours. Stir often, adding a little more water if needed.

QUICK AND EASY GUIDE TO WINES

QUICK AND EASY GUIDE TO WINES

This simple chart tells you the type of wine, where it's from, how to serve it and what foods go well with it. The foods suggested are by no means the limit of the kinds suited to the wine; they are simply an indication of where to start in matching wines and food.

Dry red wines usually are considered the best companions for cheese, but countries famous for white wines (Germany, Switzerland) serve cheese with their pale wines. In the United States, cheese sometimes is served with a sweet wine; rarely is this true elsewhere.

A *fortified* wine indicates 18 to 20 per cent alcohol content, usually.

Wines marked with (*) are generally considered to be among the great wines of the world.

WINE	TYPE	FROM	SERVE	GOOD WITH
ALEATICO Ah-lay-*ah*-tee-koh	Red dessert	*California, Italy*	*Room temp or cool*	Simple cookies, alone
ALOXE-CORTON *Ah*-loss-*Core*-tahwn	Dry red	*Burgundy*	*Room temp*	Roasts, steak, venison, duck, game, cheese
AMONTILLADO SHERRY Ah-mon-tee-*yah*-doh	Medium dry, fortified	*Spain*	*Cold or "on rocks"*	Sharp and spicy hors d'oeuvre, nuts, appetizers, soup, alone
AMOROSO SHERRY Ah-more-*oh*-so	Sweet, amber, fortified	*Spain*	*Room temp or cool*	Nuts, simple cakes, cookies, alone
ANGELICA Ahn-*jell*-ee-kah	Very sweet, golden	*California*	*Room temp*	Nuts, fruit, alone
ASTI SPUMANTE *Ahs*-tee Spoo-*mahn*-tee	Semi-sweet, white, sparkling	*Italy*	*Cold*	Desserts of all kinds
*AUSONE, CHATEAU *Oh*-sohn	Dry red	*Bordeaux*	*Room temp*	All meats (especially beef), roast turkey, duck cheese
BARBARESCO Bar-bah-*rez*-coe	Dry red	*Italy*	*Room temp*	Roasts, game, chops, spaghetti, chili, curry, hamburgers, cheese
BARBERA Bar-*beh*-rah	Dry red	*Italy*	*Room temp*	Spaghetti, chili, curry, pizza, strong-flavored dishes, barbecue, cheese
BARDOLINO Bar-doh-*leen*-oh	Dry red, light	*Italy*	*Room temp*	Beef, veal, lamb, pork, ham, cold cuts, omelets, cheese
BAROLO Bah-*ro*-lo	Dry red	*Italy*	*Room temp*	Roasts, game, spicy dishes, sausage, rich stews, strong cheeses

WINE	TYPE	FROM	SERVE	GOOD WITH
BARSAC *Bar*-sock	White, sweet	*Bordeaux*	*Cool*	Pastry, cakes, alone (sometimes with rich sea food)
BEAUJOLAIS Bo-zho-lay	Dry red	*Burgundy*	*Cool*	Barbecue and picnic foods, especially beef, ham, fried chicken, cheese
BEAUNE Bone	Dry red	*Burgundy*	*Room temp*	Roasts, steak, chops, game, robust dishes, cheese
BERNKASTELER *Barn*-kahst-ler	Dry white	*Moselle*	*Cold*	Fish, sea food, chicken, veal, cold cuts, omelets, bland foods
*BERNKASTELER DOKTOR *Barn*-kahst-ler *Dok*-tore	Dry white	*Moselle*	*Cold*	Fish, sea food, chicken, veal, cold cuts, omelets, bland foods
BLANC DE BLANCS Blahn duh Blahn	Dry white	*Champagne*	*Cold*	Dainty sandwiches, cakes, bland and festive foods
BURGUNDY *Bur*-gun-dee	Dry red	*California, New York, other U.S.*	*Room temp or cool*	All meats (especially beef), game, cheese
CABERNET SAUVIGNON Cab-er-nay So-vee-nyohn	Dry red, Claret	*California*	*Room temp or cool*	Beef, veal, pork, ham, lamb, steak, chops, cheese
CAPRI *Kah*-pree	Dry white	*Italy*	*Cold*	Fish, sea food, veal, chicken, spaghetti with clam sauce or mushrooms

WINE	*TYPE*	*FROM*	*SERVE*	*GOOD WITH*
CATAWBA Kuh-*taw*-bah	Semi-sweet white, pink	*New York, Ohio*	*Cold*	Desserts, fruit, cookies or cake, alone
CHABLIS, FRENCH *Shah*-blee	Dry white	*Burgundy*	*Cold*	Sea food (especially oysters, fish), chicken, veal, lamb
CHABLIS, U.S. *Shah*-blee	Medium dry, white	*California, New York, other U.S.*	*Cold*	Fish, sea food, chicken, lamb, veal, egg and cheese dishes
*CHAMBERTIN, LE Luh-*Shahm*-ber-tan	Dry red	*Burgundy*	*Room temp*	Roasts, steak, venison, duck, game, cheese
CHAMBOLLE MUSIGNY *Shahm*-bowl *Moo*-see-knee	Dry red	*Burgundy*	*Room temp*	Roasts, steak, venison, duck, game, cheese
CHAMPAGNE Shahm-*pain*	Dry to semi-sweet, white, red, pink	*Champagne, California, New York, other U.S.*	*Cold*	Appetizers, chicken, turkey, desserts, cakes, any festive foods
CHARBONO Shar-*bo*-no	Dry red	*California*	*Room temp*	Spaghetti, hamburgers, ham, chops, steak, cheese
CHARDONNAY Shar-doh-*nay*	Dry white, Chablis	*California*	*Cold*	Sea food (especially oysters), fish, veal, chicken, turkey, lamb
CHASSAGNE-MONTRACHET *Shah*-sign-*Moan*-rah-shay	Dry white	*Burgundy*	*Cold*	Dover sole, delicate fish, sea food, veal, chicken, turkey, ham, lamb
CHATEAUNEUF-DU-PAPE Shot-oh-*nuf*-due-Pop	Dry red	*Rhône*	*Room temp or cool*	Beef, stews, game, steak, pot roast, chicken, ham, cheese

WINE	TYPE	FROM	SERVE	GOOD WITH
CHENIN BLANC *She*-nin Blahn	Dry to sweet, white	*California*	*Cold*	Dry—fish, sea food, veal, chicken. Sweet—desserts
*CHEVAL BLANC, CHATEAU *Shev*-ahl Blahn	Dry red	*Bordeaux*	*Room temp*	Roasts, steak, chops, lamb, game, cheese
CHIANTI Kee-*ahn*-tee	Dry red	*Italy*	*Room temp*	Spaghetti, chili, hamburgers, spicy foods, cheese
CHINON She-*nohn*	Dry red, light	*France*	*Cool*	Veal, chicken, cold cuts, ham, pork, lamb, casseroles, cheese
CLARET *Klair*-et	Dry red	*California, other U.S.*	*Room temp or cool*	Beef, pork, ham, lamb, stews, game, cheese
*CLOS DE TART Klo duh *Tar*	Dry red	*Burgundy*	*Room temp*	Roasts, steak, chops, venison, game, cheese
CLOS DE VOUGEOT Klo duh *Voo*-zho	Dry red	*Burgundy*	*Room temp*	Roasts, steak, chops, ham, duck, venison, cheese
CLOS DES LAMBRAYS Klo day Lahm-*bray*	Dry red	*Burgundy*	*Room temp*	Roasts, steak, chops, venison, game, cheese
CLOS ST. DENIS Klo San *Denny*	Dry red	*Burgundy*	*Room temp*	Roasts, steak, chops, ham, duck, venison, cheese
*CORTON, LE Luh Core-*tawn*	Dry red	*Burgundy*	*Room temp*	Roasts, steak, chops, ham, duck, venison, cheese
*CORTON-CHARLEMAGNE Core-*tawn*-*Shar*-luh-main	Dry red	*Burgundy*	*Room temp*	Roasts, steak, chops, ham, duck, venison, cheese
COTE DE BEAUNE Coat duh *Bone*	Dry red	*Burgundy*	*Room temp*	Roasts, steak, chops, ham, duck, venison, cheese

WINE	TYPE	FROM	SERVE	GOOD WITH
COTES DE PROVENCE Coat duh Pro-*vahns*	Dry pink	*France*	*Cold*	Luncheon dishes, sea food, cold cuts, all foods
COTE ROTIE Coat Wrote-*ee*	Dry red	*Rhône*	*Room temp or cool*	Beef, ham, roasts, steak, chicken, turkey, duck, cheese
COTES DU RHONE Coat due *Rone*	Dry red or pink	*Rhône*	*Room temp or chilled*	Beef, veal, lamb, ham, pork, cheese. Pink—all foods
DEIDESHEIMER *Die*-dehs-high-mer	Dry white	*Rhine*	*Cold*	Fish, sea food, cold cuts, chicken, turkey, veal, eggs
DELAWARE	Dry to sweet	*New York*	*cool* *Cold or*	Veal, fish, chicken, cold cuts. Sweet—pastry, cakes
DÉZALEY *Day*-zah-lay	Dry white	*Switzerland*	*Cold*	Fish, sea food, veal, chicken, turkey, lamb, fondue, omelets
DIAMOND, MOORE'S	Dry white	*New York*	*Cold*	Fish, sea food, chicken, turkey, veal, casseroles
DIANA	Dry white	*New York*	*Cold*	Fish, sea food, chicken, turkey, veal, casseroles
D'ISSAN, CHATEAU Dee-*sahn*	Dry red	*Bordeaux*	*Room temp*	Beef roasts, steaks, lamb, duck, cheese
DOLE DU VALAIS Dole dew Vah-*lay*	Dry red	*Switzerland*	*Room temp*	All meats, spicy foods, cheese
DUBONNET Dew-bow-*nay*	Sweet red, fortified, quinined	*France, California*	*Cold*	Hors d'oeuvres, alone (also used in cocktails)

WINE	TYPE	FROM	SERVE	GOOD WITH
DUTCHESS	Dry white	*New York*	*Cold*	Fish, sea food, veal, chicken, casseroles, cold cuts, omelets
ÉCHEZEAUX *Eh*-shehs-oh	Dry red	*Burgundy*	*Room temp*	Roasts, game, cheese
ELVIRA El-*vee*-ra	Dry white	*New York*	*Cold*	Fish, sea food, veal, chicken
EMERALD DRY RIESLING *Rees*-ling	Dry white	*California*	*Cold*	Fish, sea food, lamb, ham, cold cuts, chicken, casseroles
EST! EST!! EST!!!	Dry to sweet, white	*Italy*	*Cold*	Fish, sea food, veal, chicken. Sweet—pastry, cakes
FALERNO Fah-*lair*-no	Dry red or white	*Italy*	*Room temp or cold*	Beef, pork, stews, cheese. White—fish, sea food, veal
FENDANT *Fahn*-dawn	Dry white	*Switzerland*	*Cold*	Fish, sea food, veal, chicken, fondue, cheese dishes
FINO SHERRY *Feen*-oh	Pale dry	*Spain*	*Cold or "on rocks"*	Appetizers (especially spicy and sharp), nuts
FIXIN Feex-*ahn*	Dry red	*Burgundy*	*Room temp*	Roasts, steak, venison, duck, game, cheese
FOLLE BLANCHE Fohl *Blahnsh*	Dry white, Chablis	*California*	*Cold*	Fish, sea food, veal, turkey, chicken, egg and cheese dishes
FORSTER *Forst*-er	Dry white	*Germany*	*Cold*	Fish, sea food, veal, turkey, chicken, egg and cheese dishes

WINE	TYPE	FROM	SERVE	GOOD WITH
FRANKEN RIESLING or SYLVANER *Sil*-vah-nur	Dry white	*California, Rhine*	*Cold*	Sea food, fish, veal, turkey, chicken, cheese, egg and cheese dishes
FRASCATI Frahs-*kah*-tee	Dry to medium dry, white	*Italy*	*Cold*	Sea food, fish, veal, turkey, chicken, cheese, egg and cheese dishes, pastas made with sea food
FREISA *Fray*-za	Dry or sweet, red	*Italy*	*Room temp*	Roasts, pot roasts, spaghetti. Sweet—desserts
GAMAY or GAMAY BEAUJOLAIS Ga-*may*	Dry red	*California*	*Cool or cold*	Beef roasts, pot roasts, stews, ham, hamburgers, casseroles, cheese
GEVREY-CHAMBERTIN *Zhev*-ray-*Shahm*-ber-tahn	Dry red	*Burgundy*	*Room temp*	Roasts, steak, chops, game, duck, cheese
GEWÜRZ-TRAMINER Geh-*wurtz*-trah-*meen*-er	Dry white	*France, Germany, California*	*Cold*	Fish, shellfish, veal, chicken, turkey, cold cuts, omelets
GRAGNANO Grah-*nyá*-no	Dry red	*Italy*	*Room temp*	Beef roasts, stews, barbecue, spaghetti, cheese
*GRANDS ÉCHEZEAUX, LES Luh Grahnz *Eh*-sheh-zoh	Dry red	*Burgundy*	*Room temp*	Roasts, steak, venison, duck, game, cheese
GRAVES Grahv	Dry to medium dry, white	*Bordeaux*	*Cold*	Fish, sea food, veal, chicken, turkey, egg and cheese dishes
GREEN HUNGARIAN	Dry white	*California*	*Cold*	Fish, shellfish, veal, chicken, turkey, casseroles
GRENACHE ROSÉ Gren-*ahsh* Ro-*zay*	Dry pink	*California*	*Cold*	All foods (especially light dishes, spicy fare, sea food, ham)

WINE	TYPE	FROM	SERVE	GOOD WITH
GREY RIESLING *Rees*-ling	Dry white	*California*	*Cold*	Fish, shellfish, veal, ham, lamb, cold cuts, cheese dishes
GRIGNOLINO Green-yo-*leen*-oh	Dry red	*Italy, California*	*Room temp*	Roasts, pot roasts, hamburgers, spaghetti, casseroles, cheese
HALLGARTENER *Hahl*-gart-ner	Dry or sweet	*Germany*	*Cold*	Fish, shellfish, veal, chicken, lamb. Sweet—desserts
*HAUT-BRION, CHATEAU Oh-Bree-*awn*	Dry red	*Bordeaux*	*Room temp*	Roasts, steak, game, pork, ham, cheese
HAUT SAUTERNE Oh So-*turn*	Semi-sweet white	*California, New York*	*Cold*	Fish, shellfish, veal, chicken, luncheon dishes
HAUT SAUTERNES Oh So-*turn*	Sweet white	*Bordeaux*	*Cold*	Pastry, sweets
HERMITAGE *Ere*-me-tahzh	Dry red and white	*Rhône*	*Room temp or cold*	Red—roasts, game, cheese. White—fish, sea food, veal
HOCHHEIMER *Hock*-high-mer	Dry white	*Rhine*	*Cold*	Fish, sea food, veal, chicken, lamb, cold cuts, bland foods, cheese
HOCHHEIMER KIRCHENSTUCK *Keerk*-hen-styck	Dry white	*Rhine*	*Cold*	Fish, sea food, ve chicken, lamb, cold cuts, blanc foods, cheese
HOSPICES DE BEAUNE *Awes*-piece duh *Bone*	Dry red	*Burgundy*	*Room temp*	Roasts (especially beef), steak, game, cheese

WINE	TYPE	FROM	SERVE	GOOD WITH
INFERNO Een-*fair*-no	Dry red	*Italy*	*Room temp*	Roasts, steak, chops, game, stews, curries, sausage, Italian cheeses
*JOHANNISBERG, SCHLOSS Schloss Yo-*hann*-is-burg	Dry white	*Germany*	*Cold*	Fish, sea food, veal, chicken, lamb, ham, egg dishes, cold cuts, cheese
JOHANNISBERG(ER) RIESLING Yo-*hann*-is-burg *Rees*-ling	Dry white	*California, Germany*	*Cold*	Fish, sea food, veal, chicken, lamb, ham, egg dishes, cold cuts, cheese
KOKINELLI Ko-kee-*nell*-ee	Dry red, resined	*Greece*	*Cold*	Greek dishes (not generally appealin to uninitiated)
LACRIMA CHRISTI *Lah*-cream-ah *Crease*-tea	Semi-dry white	*Italy*	*Cold*	Cold dishes, chicken, turkey, rich or smoked fish, pastry
*LAFITE-ROTHSCHILD, CHATEAU Lah-*feet*-*Row*-shield	Dry red	*Bordeaux*	*Room temp*	Roasts, steak, chops, game, roast turkey, ham, duck, cheese
LAMBRUSCO Lahm-*broo*-skoh	Dry or semi-dry, red	*Italy*	*Cool*	Sausage, ham, pork, beef, duck, spaghetti, rice dishes
LASCOMBES, CHATEAU *Lahs*-comb	Dry red	*Bordeaux*	*Room temp*	Beef, lamb, ham, pork, game, duck, cheese
*LATOUR, CHATEAU Lah-*toor*	Dry red	*Bordeaux*	*Room temp*	Beef, lamb, ham, pork, game, duck, cheese
LAUBENHEIMER Lau-ben-high-mur	Dry white	*Rhine*	*Cold*	Fish, sea food, veal, chicken, egg and cheese dishes
LAVAUX Lah-vo	Dry white	*Switzerland*	*Cold*	Fish, sea food, veal, chicken, egg and cheese dishes

WINE	TYPE	FROM	SERVE	GOOD WITH
LIEBFRAUMILCH *Leeb*-frau-milsh	Dry white	*Rhine*	*Cold*	Fish, sea food, chicken, veal, cold cuts, light foods
LIRAC *Lee*-rock	Pink	*Rhône*	*Cold*	All foods (especially light fare, summer dishes)
LUGANA Loo-*gah*-nah	Dry white	*Italy*	*Cold*	Fish, sea food, light meats
MADEIRA Mah-*day*-rah	Dry to sweet, fortified	*Portugal*	*Cold or room temp*	Dry—appetizers (especially spicy). Sweet—nuts, fruit
MALAGA *Mah*-lah-gah	Sweet, dark, fortified	*Spain*	*Room temp or cool*	Desserts, fruit, nuts, cheese
MALMSEY *Mahm*-zee	Sweet, dark, fortified	*Portugal*	*Room temp or cool*	Desserts, fruit, nuts, cheese
MALVASIA Mahl-vah-*zee*-ah	Sweet, golden	*Italy*	*Room temp or cool*	Desserts, fruit, nuts, cheese
MANZANILLA SHERRY Mahn-tha-*nee*-yah	Very dry, straw-color, fortified	*Spain*	*Cold or "on rocks"*	Spicy, salty appetizers, smoked foods, cheese dips
MARCOBRUNNER *Mahr*-coe-bruhn-er	Dry white	*Germany*	*Cold*	Dover sole, turbot, other fine fish, shellfish, lamb, veal, chicken
*MARGAUX, CHATEAU Mar-go	Dry red	*Bordeaux*	*Room temp*	Roasts, steak, chops, meats with sauces, cheese
MARSALA Mar-*sah*-lah	Sweet, brown	*Sicily*	*Room temp*	Nuts, fruit, desserts, alone
MAVRODAPHNE Mahv-row-*dahf*-neh	Sweet red, fortified	*Greece*	*Room temp*	Nuts, fruit, desserts, alone

WINE	TYPE	FROM	SERVE	GOOD WITH
MAY WINE	Semi-sweet white	*Germany*	*Cold*	Cookies, pastry, little cakes (used in punch bowl with fruit)
MEDOC May-dock	Dry red	*Bordeaux*	*Room temp*	Roasts, steak, game, meats with sauces, cheese
MERLOT *Mare*-low	Dry red	*Switzerland*	*Room temp*	Roasts, steak, chops, cold cuts, casseroles, cheese
MEURSAULT *Mere*-so	Dry white	*Burgundy*	*Cold*	Fish, sea food, veal, lamb, roast turkey
*MONTRACHET *Moan*-rah-shay	Dry white	*Burgundy*	*Cold*	Fish, sea food, veal, lamb, roast turkey
MOREY-ST. DENIS Mo-ray-San-duh-*nee*	Dry red	*Burgundy*	*Room temp*	Beef, game, poultry, roasts
MOSCATO Mos-*kah*-toe	Sweet, golden, fortified	*Italy*	*Room temp*	Fruit, nuts, simple cakes, desserts, alone
MOSELBLÜMCHEN *Mo*-zel-bluhm-shen	Dry white	*Moselle*	*Cold*	Fish, sea food, light meats, lamb, cold chicken, ham
MOSELLE *Mo*-zel	Dry white	*Germany*	*Cold*	Fish, sea food, omelets, lamb, chicken, veal
MOULIN-A-VENT *Moo*-lan-ah-Vahn	Light, dry red	*Burgundy*	*Cool*	Ham, lamb, chicken, beef, stews, hamburger, cheese
*MOUTON-ROTHSCHILD, CHATEAU *Moo*-tawn-*Ro*-shield	Dry red	*Bordeaux*	*Room temp*	Roasts, steak, chops, ham, spicy dishes, cheese
MUSCAT FRONTIGNAN *Moos*-kah *Frawn*-tee-nyon	Sweet, golden, fortified	*France, California*	*Room temp*	Fruit, nuts, simple cakes, alone

WINE	TYPE	SERVE	FROM	GOOD WITH
MUSCATEL Muss-kah-*tell*	Sweet, golden, fortified	*U.S.*	*Room temp*	Fruit, nuts, simple cakes, alone
*MUSIGNY, LE Luh *Mew*-see-knee	Dry red	*Burgundy*	*Room temp*	Beef roasts, steak, chops, game, duck, cheese
NEBBIOLO Nehb-bee-*oh*-low	Medium sweet, red	*Italy, Switzerland*	*Room temp or cool*	Pastry, nuts, fruit, cheese, alone
NEUCHATEL New-shah-*tell*	Dry white	*Switzerland*	*Cold*	Sea food, cold cuts, ham, meat salads, pastry, nuts
NIAGARA	Semi-dry, white	*New York*	*Cold*	Sea food, cold cuts, ham, meat salads, pastry, nuts
NIERSTEINER *Near*-shtine-er	Dry white	*Germany*	*Cold*	Sea food, cold cuts, ham, meat salads, pastry, nuts
NUITS ST. GEORGES *Nwee* San *Jorj*	Dry red	*Burgundy*	*Room temp*	Roasts, steak, venison, game, highly seasoned dishes, cheese
OEIL DE PERDRIX Oy duh *Pear*-dree	Dry pink	*Burgundy, Switzerland*	*Cold*	All foods (especially sea food, cold chicken, turkey, light luncheon dishes)
OLIVIER, CHATEAU *Oh*-lee-vee-ay	Dry red	*Bordeaux*	*Room temp*	Roasts, poultry, game, ham, cheese
OLOROSO SHERRY Oh-lo-*ro*-so	Sweet, golden	*Spain*	*Cool or room temp*	Nuts, fruit, wafers, alone
OPPENHEIMER Oppen-*high*-mur	Dry white	*Rhine*	*Cold*	Fish, sea food, veal, lamb, ham, chicken

WINE	TYPE	FROM	SERVE	GOOD WITH
ORVIETO Or-vee-*et*-oh	Dry or sweet, white or pink	*Italy*	*Cold*	Dry, white—fish, sea food. Pink—all foods. Sweet—pastry, desserts
PAUILLAC *Poy*-yock	Dry red	*Bordeaux*	*Room temp*	Roasts (especially beef), steak, poultry, game, cheese
*PÉTRUS, CHATEAU *Peh*-trews	Dry red	*Bordeaux*	*Room temp*	Roasts, steak, chops, venison, game, cheese
PIESPORTER *Peas*-porter	Dry white	*Moselle*	*Cold*	Fish, sea food, veal, chicken, turkey, cold buffet foods
PINOT BLANC *Pea*-no Blahn	Dry white	*California*	*Cold*	Fish, sea food, veal, chicken, turkey, cold buffet foods
PINOT CHARDONNAY *Pea*-no Shar-doh-*nay*	Dry white	*California*	*Cold*	Sea food (especially oysters, lobster), chicken, turkey, veal
PINOT NOIR *Pea*-no Nwahr	Dry red	*California*	*Room temp*	Roasts, steak, chops, game, cheese (a Burgundy-type wine)
POMEROL *Poe*-mer-all	Dry red	*Bordeaux*	*Room temp*	Roasts, steak, chops, game, duck, cheese
POMMARD *Poe*-mahr	Dry red	*Burgundy*	*Room temp*	Roasts, steak, chops, game, duck, cheese
PORT	Sweet, red or tawny	*Portugal, U.S.*	*Room temp*	Cheese, nuts, fruit, plain cake, alone
POUILLY-FUISSÉ P*wee*-yee-Fwee-*say*	Dry white	*Burgundy*	*Cold*	Fish, sea food, chicken, veal, turkey, omelets, cheese dishes

WINE	TYPE	FROM	SERVE	GOOD WITH
POUILLY FUMÉ *Pwee*-yee Foo-*may*	Dry white	*France*	*Cold*	Fish, sea food (especially oysters), chicken, veal, turkey, omelets, cheese dishes
POUILLY SUR LOIRE *Pwee*-yee sir *Lwahr*	Dry white	*France*	*Cold*	Fish, sea food (especially oysters), chicken, veal, turkey, omelets, cheese dishes
PRIEURÉ-LICHINE, CHATEAU Pree-you-*ray*-Luh-*sheen*	Dry red	*Bordeaux*	*Room temp*	Roasts, steak, chops, game, duck, cheese
PULIGNY-MONTRACHET *Pool*-ee-nee-*Moan*-rah-shay	Dry white	*Burgundy*	*Cold*	Fish, sea food veal, chicken, turkey, lamb, ham
QUINCY *Kehn*-see	Dry white	*France*	*Cold*	Fish, sea food, veal, chicken, turkey, lamb, ham
RETSINA Ret-*see*-nah	Dry red, resined	*Greece*	*Cool or room temp*	Greek foods (not generally pleasing to uninitiated)
RHINE WINE	Dry white	*Germany, U.S.*	*Cold*	Fish, sea food, veal, ham, lamb, chicken, turkey
*RICHEBOURG *Reesh*-boorg	Dry red	*Burgundy*	*Room temp*	Roasts, steak, chops, game (especially venison), cheese
RIESLING *Rees*-ling	Dry white	*Germany, France, U.S.*	*Cold*	Fish, sea food, veal, ham, chicken, lamb
RIOJA Ree-*oh*-ha	Dry red	*Spain*	*Room temp or cold*	Beef, pork, ham, sausage, cheese, casseroles (used in recipe for Sangria, page xx)

WINE	TYPE	FROM	SERVE	GOOD WITH
*ROMANÉE, LA Lah Rome-ah-*nay*	Dry red	*Burgundy*	*Room temp*	Roasts, steak, chops, game, cheese
*ROMANÉE CONTI Rome-ah-*nay* Kawn-*tee*	Dry red	*Burgundy*	*Room temp*	Roasts, steak, chops, game, cheese
ROSÉ Ro-*zay*	Dry or semi-sweet, pink	*All countries*	*Cold*	All foods (especially sea food, light dishes)
ROSÉ D'ANJOU Ro-*zay* *dahn*-zhoo	Dry to semi-sweet, pink	*France*	*Cold*	All foods (especially light dishes, sea food, casseroles, chicken)
ROSÉ D'ARBOIS Ro-*zay* *dar*-bwa	Dry pink	*France*	*Cold*	All foods (especially light dishes, sea food, casseroles, chicken)
RÜDESHEIMER *Rue*-des-high-mur	Dry white	*Rhine*	*Cold*	Fish, sea food, veal, lamb, chicken, light dishes
ST. ÉMILION San-teh-mee-lee-*awn*	Dry red	*Bordeaux*	*Room temp*	Roasts, steak, chops, duck, ham, game, cheese
ST. ESTEPHE San-teh-*stef*	Dry red	*Bordeaux*	*Room temp*	Roasts (especially beef), steak, ham, lamb, pork, cheese
ST. JULIEN San-zhoo-*lee*-en	Dry red	*Bordeaux*	*Room temp*	Roasts (especially beef), steak, ham, lamb, pork, cheese
STE. ROSELINE, CHATEAU San-Rohz-ah-*leen*	Dry pink	*France*	*Cold*	All foods (especially light dishes, sea food, casseroles, chicken)

WINE	TYPE	FROM	SERVE	GOOD WITH
SAMOS, MUSCAT OF *Say*-muss	Sweet, golden	*Greece*	*Room temp*	Desserts, fruit, nuts, alone
SANCERRE *Sahn*-sehr	Dry white	*France*	*Cold*	Sea food, fish, chicken, veal, turkey, lamb, ham, egg and cheese dishes
SANGIOVESE Sahn-gee-oh-*veh*-seh	Dry red	*Italy*	*Room temp*	Beef, pork, spicy dishes, curries, sausage, cheese
SANSEVERO San-*seh*-veh-row	Dry white	*Italy*	*Cold*	Fish, sea food, veal, pork, spaghetti, rice dishes
SANTENAY Sahn-tah-*nay*	Dry red	*Burgundy*	*Room temp or cool*	Roasts, steak, chops, game, cheese
SAUMUR So-mure	Semi-sweet, white or pink	*France*	*Cold*	Fish, sea food, light luncheon dishes, chicken, pastry. Pink—all foods
SAUTERNE So-*turn*	Dry to semi-sweet	*U.S.*	*Cold*	Fish, sea food, light luncheon dishes. Sweeter—with pastry
SAUTERNES So-*turn*	Sweet	*Bordeaux*	*Cold*	Pastry, desserts, sometimes salmon, other rich fish
SAUVIGNON BLANC So-vee-nyohn Blahn	Dry to sweet, white	*California*	*Cold*	Fish, sea food, light luncheon dishes, chicken
*SCHLOSS VOLLRADS Shloss *Fall*-rods	Dry white	*Rhine*	*Cold*	Fish, sea food, veal, chicken, turkey, lamb, ham, cold meats, cheese dishes
SCUPPERNONG *Skup*-er-nong	Sweet white	*U.S. (southeast)*	*Cool*	Nuts, fruit, desserts, alone

WINE	TYPE	FROM	SERVE	GOOD WITH
SEMILLON Say-me-*yohn*	Dry or sweet, white	*California*	*Cold*	Fish, sea food, white meats. Sweet—pastry, fruit, cakes
SERCIAL MADEIRA *Sir*-see-ahl Mah-*day*-rah	Dry, pale straw-colored, fortified	*Portugal*	*Cold*	Appetizers (especially spicy ones), alone before a meal
SHERRY, SPANISH	Dry to sweet, fortified	*Spain*	*Cold or room temp*	Dry—appetizers (especially spicy ones), alone. Sweet—nuts, fruit, alone
SHERRY, U.S.	Dry to sweet, pale amber, fortified	*U.S.*	*Cold or room temp*	Dry—appetizers (especially spicy ones), alone. Sweet—nuts, fruit, alone
SMITH-HAUT-LAFITTE, CHATEAU Smeet-oh-Lah-*feet*	Dry red	*Bordeaux*	*Room temp*	Roasts, steak, chops, game, cheese
SOAVE So-*ah*-veh	Dry white	*Italy*	*Cold*	Fish, sea food, veal, chicken, egg and cheese dishes
SPARKLING BURGUNDY	Semi-sweet red	*France, U.S.*	*Cold*	Beef, stews, barbecue, ham, pork, duck, cheese
STEINWEIN Stine-wine	Dry white	*Germany*	*Cold*	Fish, sea food, veal, chicken, casseroles, cold cuts
SYLVANER, or FRANKEN RIESLING *Sil*-vah-nur	Dry white	*California*	*Cold*	Fish, sea food, veal, chicken, casseroles, cold cuts
SZAMORODNI Zhah-more-*od*-knee	Semi-sweet to sweet, white	*Hungary*	*Room temp*	Desserts, fruit, cakes, alone
*TACHE, LA Lah *Tahsh*	Dry red	*Burgundy*	*Room temp*	Roasts, venison, game, duck, cheese

WINE	*TYPE*	*FROM*	*SERVE*	*GOOD WITH*
TARRAGONA Tahr-ah-*go*-nah	Sweet red	*Spain*	*Room temp*	Nuts, fruit, cheese, fruit cake
TAVEL Tah-*vell*	Dry pink	*France*	*Cold*	All foods (especially light luncheon dishes, curries, fish)
TOKAY, HUNGARIAN	Semi-sweet to sweet, golden	*Hungary*	*Room temp*	Desserts, fruit, nuts, alone
TOKAY, U.S.	Sweet golden	*U.S.*	*Cool or room temp*	Desserts, fruit, nuts, alone
TRAMINER, or GEWÜRZTRAMINER Trah-*meen*-er	Dry white	*France, Germany, California*	*Cold*	Fish, shellfish, veal, chicken, turkey, cold cuts, omelets
VALDEPENAS Val-de-*pay*-nyas	Dry red	*Spain*	*Room temp*	Beef roasts, steak, pork, ham, duck, game
VALPENTENA Val-pen-*tay*-nah	Dry red	*Italy*	*Room temp*	All meats, spaghetti, rice dishes, cheese, casseroles
VALPOLICELLA Val-pol-lee-*cheh*-lah	Dry red	*Italy*	*Room temp*	All meats, spaghetti, rice dishes, cheese, casseroles
VALTELLINA Val-tel-*lee*-nah	Dry red	*Italy*	*Room temp*	All meats, spaghetti, rice dishes, cheese, casseroles
VERDICCHIO Ver-*deek*-yoh	Dry or semi-dry, white	*Italy*	*Cold*	Fish, sea food, veal, cold cuts, chicken, ham, lamb, spaghetti

WINE	TYPE	FROM	SERVE	GOOD WITH
VERMOUTH	Dry or sweet, red or white	*Italy, France, U.S.*	*Chilled or "on rocks"*	Dry—appetizers. Sweet—desserts. Either with fish, in mixed drinks, alone
VERNACCIA Ver-*nah*-chee-ah	Dry, amber, strong	*Italy*	*Cold*	Fish, alone
VESUVIO Veh-*soo*-vee-oh	Dry red	*Italy*	*Room temp*	Spicy dishes with tomato, spaghetti, hamburgers, cheese
VIN SANTO Veen *San*-toe	Sweet white	*Italy*	*Room temp*	Desserts, fruit, cakes, nuts, cheese
VOIGNY, CHATEAU V*wa*-nyee	Sweet white	*Bordeaux*	*Cold*	Desserts, sometimes with salmon, trout, sea food, smoked fish
VOUVRAY V*oov*-ray	Semi-sweet white	*France*	*Cold*	Fish, sea food, chicken, veal, omelets, pastry
WACHENHEIMER W*ok*-en-high-mur	Dry white	*Germany*	*Cold*	Fish, sea food, chicken, veal, omelets, ham, lamb, cold cuts
WHITE PORT	Sweet white	*Spain, U.S.*	*Cold*	Desserts, nuts, fruit, cakes, alone
*YQUEM, CHATEAU D' *Ee*-calm	Sweet white	*Bordeaux*	*Cold or cool*	Desserts, pastry, sometimes with sea food, salmon, rich fish dishes
ZELLER SCHWARZE KATZ	Dry white	*Moselle*	*Cold*	Fish, sea food, light meats, lamb, cold chicken, ham
ZINFANDEL Z*in*-fan-dell	Dry red	*California*	*Room temp or cool*	All meats, pot roasts, hamburgers, cold cuts, spaghetti, cheese

SOME RECOMMENDED BOOKS ON WINE AND COOKING WITH WINE

This is only a beginning, as there are dozens of good books. I have confined the list to the less expensive, general interest volumes, many of them packed with good information.

LEON D. ADAMS, *The Commonsense Book of Wines* (McKay)

HAROLD J. GROSSMAN, *Grossman's Guide to Wines, Spirits and Beers* (Scribner's)

WILLIAM S. LEEDOM, *The Vintage Wine Book* (Vintage Books–paperback)

ALEXIS LICHINE, *Wines of France* (Knopf)

W. E. MASSEE, *Wines and Spirits* (McGraw-Hill)

JOHN MELVILLE, *Guide to California Wines* (Nourse)

FRANK SCHOONMAKER, *The Wines of Germany* (Hastings House –paperback)

FRANK SCHOONMAKER, *Dictionary of Wines* (Hastings House)

COOKING WITH WINES:

EMILY CHASE, *The Pleasures of Cooking with Wine* (Prentice-Hall)

JEANNE OWEN, *A Wine Lover's Cook Book* (Barrows)

MORRISON WOOD, *With a Jug of Wine* (Farrar, Straus & Cudahy)

MORRISON WOOD, *More Recipes with a Jug of Wine* (Farrar, Straus & Cudahy)

Small booklets with much good information include "French Wines" by Fernande Garvin; "Imported Wines and Spirits" by Harold J. Grossman; and the "Pocket Dictionary of Wines" by Tom Marvel. These may be available free or for a small charge through your wine dealer. In addition, wine companies offer much free literature, and the publications of the California Wine Institute are helpful.

LEADING AMERICAN VINTNERS

Not all of our wines are produced in California, New York and Ohio. Wine trails lead through many other states. Most of the winemakers listed here welcome visitors, and some offer conducted tours. Summer travelers can have fun exploring the minor winegrowing regions of the country and tasting their wines. They rarely are of a quality to interest a connoisseur, but they may nevertheless be pleasant wines.

ARKANSAS

POST'S WINERY, ALTUS
table and dessert

WIEDERKEHR WINE CELLARS, ALTUS
table and dessert, fruit and berry

DE SALVO'S WINERY, CENTER RIDGE
table and dessert

FREYALDENHOVEN'S WINERY, MORRILTON
table and dessert

ALBERT NEWMAN WINERY, SCRANTON
table and berry

CENTER RIDGE WINERY, SPRINGFIELD
table and dessert

CALIFORNIA

ACAMPO WINERY & DISTILLERIES, ACAMPO
table and dessert, wine vinegar

CALIFORNIA WINE ASSOCIATION, ACAMPO

WEST SIDE WINERY, ACAMPO
table

OPICI WINERY, ALTA LOMA
table

ITALIAN SWISS COLONY (United Vintners, Inc.), ASTI (also Clovis and Stockton)
table and dessert, brandy, Vermouth, Champagne, sparkling wines and flavored wines

VINCENT LOCATELLI, BOULDER CREEK
table

POCAI AND SONS, CALISTOGA
table

SCHRAMSBERG VINEYARD COMPANY (California Champagne Corp.), CALISTOGA

JIM ABBONA WINERY, CHINO
table and dessert

BANDIERA WINES, CLOVERDALE
table and dessert

HOLLIS BLACK WINERY, CLOVERDALE
table

A. REGE WINE COMPANY, CLOVERDALE (also San Francisco)
table and dessert, Vermouth

CUCAMONGA VINEYARD COMPANY, CUCAMONGA
table and dessert, Champagne, sparkling wines, brandy, Vermouth

CUCAMONGA WINERY, CUCAMONGA
table and Vermouth

E. AND J. GALLO WINERY, CUCAMONGA
table and dessert, fruit and berry, Vermouth, special natural wines

THOMAS VINEYARDS, CUCAMONGA
table and dessert, Champagne, sparkling wines

PLACIDO BORDI, CUPERTINO (also Mountain View)
table

PICCHETTI BROTHERS, CUPERTINO
table

CALIFORNIA GROWERS WINERIES, CUTLER
dessert, brandy, special natural wines

DELANO GROWERS CO-OPERATIVE WINERY, DELANO
dessert

A. Perelli-Minetti and Sons, delano
table and dessert, brandy, concentrates

Di Giorgio Wine Company, di giorgio (also Kerman)
table and dessert, brandy, concentrates

Giumarra Vineyards Corporation, edison

Gibson Wine Company, elk grove
table and dessert, fruit and berry, Vermouth

Cadlolo Winery, escalon
table and dessert

Petri Wineries (United Vintners, Inc.), escalon
table and dessert, sparkling wines and flavored wines

Borra Winery, escondido
table and dessert

Ferarra Winery, escondido
table and dessert

Cucamonga Top Winery, etiwanda
table

Regina Grape Products Company, etiwanda
table and dessert, sparkling wines, Champagne, brandy, wine vinegar

Cadenasso Winery, fairfield
table

Hallcrest Vineyard, felton
table

James Frasinetti and Sons, florin
table and dessert

Eugene Cherpin Winery, fontana
table and dessert

Louis Cherpin Winery, fontana
table and dessert, Champagne, Vermouth

Fontana Winery, fontana
table and dessert

Liabeuf Winery, fontana
table and dessert

Bisceglia Brothers Wine Company, fresno
table and dessert, fruit wines, Champagne, Vermouth, concentrates

California Champagne Cellars, fresno
table and dessert, Champagne

Crest View Winery, fresno
table and dessert

Del Rey Co-operative Winery Association, fresno
table and dessert

Golden State Winery, fresno
table and dessert, Champagne

A. Nonini Winery, fresno
table

Roma Wine Company (Schenley Distillers, Inc.), fresno
table and dessert, Champagne, sparkling wines, brandy, Vermouth, concentrates

Nervo Winery, geyserville
table

John Pedroncelli Winery geyserville
table

Bertero Winery, gilroy
table

Bonesio Winery, gilroy
table, Champagne, Vermouth, wine vinegar

Cassa Brothers, gilroy
table

Anselmo Conrotto Winery, gilroy
table

Peter and Harry Giretti, gilroy
table

Live Oak Vineyards, gilroy
table

Virginio Pappani and Sons, gilroy
table

Solis Winery, gilroy
table

Val-Moon Winery, glen ellen
table

Brookside Vineyard Company (Assumption Abbey Winery), guasti (also Ontario)
table and dessert, Champagne, Vermouth, brandy, wine cocktails, cooking wines, altar wines, wine vinegar, concentrates

Korbel Champagne Cellars, guerneville
dessert, Champagne, sparkling wines, brandy

Santa Nella Winery, guerneville
table and dessert, Champagne, wine vinegar

PAUL RHODES WINERY, HAYWARD
table and dessert, Champagne, Vermouth

CAMBIASO WINERY AND VINEYARDS, HEALDSBURG
table

L. FOPPIANO WINE COMPANY, HEALDSBURG
table and dessert

SIMI WINERIES, HEALDSBURG
table and dessert, Champagne, sparkling wines, Vermouth

PAGANI BROTHERS, KENWOOD
table

WESTERN GRAPE PRODUCTS, KINGSBURG

CONCANNON VINEYARD, LIVERMORE
table and dessert, Champagne, sacramental

CRESTA BLANCA WINE COMPANY (Schenley Distillers, Inc.), LIVERMORE
table and dessert, Champagne, sparkling wines

WENTE BROTHERS, LIVERMORE
table

LOCKEFORD WINERY, LOCKEFORD

ALEX'S WINERY, LODI
table, Retsina, Sake-type wines

BEAR CREEK VINEYARD ASSOCIATION (Lodi Cellars of Wine Growers Guild), LODI
table and dessert, brandy, concentrates

DEL RIO WINERY, LODI

EAST-SIDE WINERY, LODI
table and dessert, brandy, Vermouth

GUILD WINE COMPANY (Wine Growers Guild), LODI
table and dessert, sparkling wines, brandy, Vermouth, concentrates

LODI WINERY, LODI
table and dessert, brandy

MID-VALLEY WINERY, LODI

RANCHO DEL OSO WINERY, LODI
table and dessert

WOODBRIDGE VINEYARD ASSOCIATION, LODI

LOOMIS WINERY, LOOMIS
table

SAN ANTONIO WINERY, LOS ANGELES
table and dessert, Vermouth

SANTA FE WINE COMPANY (United Vintners, Inc.), LOS ANGELES
table and dessert, fruit and berry, Champagne, brandy, Vermouth, aperitif and specialty wines

ALMADÉN VINEYARDS, LOS GATOS (also San Francisco)
table and dessert, Champagne, sparkling wines, brandy, Vermouth

EDWARD A. GILLICK, LOS GATOS
table

NOVITIATE OF LOS GATOS, LOS GATOS
table and dessert, sacramental

ALLIED GRAPE GROWERS (parent company of United Vintners, Inc.), MADERA
table, dessert, brandy, Vermouth, sparkling wines and flavored wines

FICKLIN VINEYARDS, MADERA
Ficklin Tinta Port

MISSION BELL WINERIES (United Vintners, Inc.), MADERA
table and dessert, brandy, Vermouth, sparkling wines and flavored wines

YOSEMITE WINERY ASSOCIATION, MADERA

BELLA NAPOLI WINERY, MANTECA
table

SAM-JASPER WINERY, MANTECA
table, special natural wines

J. E. DIGARDI WINERY, MARTINEZ
table, Vermouth, Champagne

ANTONIO FILIPPI, MIRA LOMA
table and dessert

J. FILIPPI VINTAGE COMPANY, MIRA LOMA
table and dessert

LLORDS AND ELWOOD, MISSION SAN JOSE
table and dessert, Champagne, sparkling wines

WEIBEL, MISSION SAN JOSE
table and dessert, Champagne, sparkling wines, brandy, Vermouth

EMILIO GUGLIELMO WINERY, MORGAN HILL
table

PEDRIZETTI WINERY, MORGAN HILL
table

RICHERT AND SONS, MORGAN HILL
vintage Port and Sherry, strawberry wine

GEMELLO WINERY, MOUNTAIN VIEW
table and dessert, Champagne, Vermouth

CARBONE NAPA VALLEY WINERY, NAPA
table

THE CHRISTIAN BROTHERS
(Mont La Salle Vineyards), NAPA
table and dessert, sparkling wines, brandy, Vermouth, altar wines

MAYACAMAS VINEYARDS, NAPA
table

VINELAND WINE CELLAR,
NORTH HOLLYWOOD
table and dessert, Champagne

NICHELINI VINEYARDS, OAKLAND
(also Rutherford)
table

DELTA WINERY AND DISTILLERY,
OAKVILLE
table and dessert, brandy, Vermouth

NAPA WINE COMPANY
(United Vintners, Inc.), OAKVILLE
table and dessert, sparkling wines and flavored wines

LEMOREL WINERY, OCCIDENTAL
table

JOE CANGEMI AND SON, ONTARIO
table

FOUNTAIN WINERY, ONTARIO
table and dessert

HIGHLAND WINE GROWERS, ONTARIO
table and dessert

A. GHIANDA WINERY, OROVILLE
table

MONT LA SALLE VINEYARDS
(Mt. Tivy Winery), PARLIER

NICHOLAS G. VERRY, PARLIER
table, Retsina

DUSI WINERY, PASO ROBLES
table

RUBY HILL VINEYARDS COMPANY
PLEASANTON
table

D'AGOSTINI WINERY, PLYMOUTH
table

CELLA WINERIES
(United Vintners, Inc.), REEDLEY
table

FRANZIA BROTHERS WINERY, RIPON
table and dessert, Champagne, sparkling wines, Vermouth

RUBIDOUX WINERY, RIVERSIDE
table and dessert

GARVEY WINERY, ROSEMEAD
table

BEAULIEU VINEYARD, RUTHERFORD
table and dessert, Champagne, sparkling wines, sacramental

INGLENOOK VINEYARD COMPANY,
RUTHERFORD
table and dessert

F. J. MILLER AND COMPANY,
RUTHERFORD
carbonated varietal wines

BERINGER BROTHERS, ST. HELENA
(also Napa)
table and dessert, Champagne, sparkling wines, brandy

CHRISTIAN BROTHERS WINE AND
CHAMPAGNE CELLARS, ST. HELENA

HEITZ WINE CELLAR, ST. HELENA
table, Champagne

HANNS KORNELL CELLARS, ST. HELENA
table and dessert, Champagne, sparkling wines, Vermouth

CHARLES KRUG WINERY
(C. Mondavi and Sons), ST. HELENA
table and dessert

LOUIS M. MARTINI, ST. HELENA
table and dessert

NICHELINI VINEYARD, ST. HELENA

SOUVERAIN CELLARS, ST. HELENA
table and dessert, Champagne

STONY HILL VINEYARDS, ST. HELENA
table

SUTTER HOME WINERY, ST. HELENA
table, Champagne, sparkling wines, aperitifs, Vermouth

MILLS WINERY, SACRAMENTO
table and dessert, fruit and berry, Champagne, brandy, Vermouth

CALIFORNIA GRAPE PRODUCTS
CORPORATION, SAN FRANCISCO
table and dessert, concentrates

CALIFORNIA WINE ASSOCIATION,
SAN FRANCISCO (also Lodi)
table and dessert, Champagne, sparkling wines, brandy, Vermouth, special natural wines, concentrates

MONTEBELLO WINE COMPANY, SAN FRANCISCO (also St. Helena)
table and dessert, Champagne, sparkling wines, Vermouth

VIOTTI WINERY, SAN GABRIEL
table and dessert, Champagne, sparkling wines, brandy, Vermouth

LONE HILL VINEYARDS, SAN JOSE
table and dessert, Champagne, sparkling wines, berry wines

GAETANO MANCUSO, SAN JOSE
table and dessert, Vermouth

MIRASSOU VINEYARDS, SAN JOSE
table, Champagne

SAN MARTIN VINEYARDS COMPANY SAN MARTIN
table and dessert, fruit wines, Champagne, Vermouth, wine vinegar

SANGER WINERY ASSOCIATION, SANGER

BRANGER VINEYARD, SANTA ROSA
table

MARTINI AND PRATI WINES, SANTA ROSA
table and dessert, fruit wines, Champagne, sparkling Burgundy, Vermouth

SANTA ROSA WINERY, SANTA ROSA
table, Champagne, sparkling wines

PAUL MASSON VINEYARDS, SARATOGA
table and dessert, Champagne, sparkling wines, brandy, Vermouth

MARTIN RAY, SARATOGA
table, Champagne

SELMA WINERY, SELMA
dessert, grape and fruit brandy, concentrates

BUENA VISTA VINEYARDS, SONOMA
table and dessert

SAMUELE SEBASTIANI, SONOMA
table and dessert, varietal wines, Vermouth, Champagne

BARGETTO'S SANTA CRUZ WINERY, SOQUEL
table

NICASIO VINEYARDS, SOQUEL
table, Champagne

PELLEGRINI BROTHERS WINERY, SOUTH SAN FRANCISCO
table and dessert, Champagne, Vermouth

WOODEN VALLEY WINERY, SUISUN
table and dessert, Vermouth

PESENTI WINERY, TEMPLETON
table

ROTTA WINERY, TEMPLETON
table

TIBURON VINEYARDS, TIBURON
table

PARDUCCI WINE CELLARS, UKIAH
table and dessert, sparkling wines, Vermouth

VICTOR WINERY, VICTOR
table and dessert

S. MARTINELLI AND COMPANY, WATSONVILLE

OLD MILL WINERY, WHITTIER
table and dessert, Vermouth

WINDSOR FARM ASSOCIATES, WINDSOR (also San Francisco)
table

DEL RIO WINERY (Wine Growers Guild), WOODBRIDGE (also Lodi)
table and dessert, brandy, Vermouth

CONNECTICUT

HEUBLEIN, INC., HARTFORD
Vermouth

VINCENT BUONOCORE AND SONS, NEW HAVEN
table and dessert, fruit and berry, Vermouth

FLORIDA

BARTELS WINERY, PENSACOLA (also Elberta, Alabama)
table, fruit wines, Scuppernong

GEORGIA

MONARCH WINE COMPANY, ATLANTA
dessert, fruit wines, Vermouth

ILLINOIS

KAPLAN'S WINERY CORPORATION, CHICAGO
kosher sweet wine

LOMBARDO WINE COMPANY, CHICAGO
table and dessert, fruit and berry

MOGEN DAVID WINE CORPORATION, CHICAGO
table, fruit wines, brandy

NISHKIAN WINE COMPANY, CHICAGO
table and dessert

PACIFIC WINE COMPANY, CHICAGO
table and dessert, Champagne, sparkling wines, Vermouth, fruit brandy

D. RECHER AND COMPANY, CHICAGO
table and dessert, Champagne, sparkling wines, brandy, Vermouth, American May wine

GEM CITY VINELAND COMPANY, NAUVOO
table and dessert

IOWA

OLD WINE CELLAR WINERY, AMANA
table

COUNCIL BLUFFS GRAPE GROWERS ASSOCIATION, COUNCIL BLUFFS
table and dessert

DIAMOND J. WINERY, FORT MADISON
table and dessert

EHRLE BROTHERS WINERY, HOMESTEAD
grape and rhubarb wine

NEW MELLERAY ABBEY, PEOSTA
sacramental

KENTUCKY

MONTE CASSINO WINE COMPANY, COVINGTON
dessert, fruit wines

LOUISIANA

ALBERT KAPOTSKY WINERY, LEESVILLE
table and dessert

LULICH BROTHERS, TRIUMPH
table, orange wine

MAINE

FAIRVIEW WINE COMPANY, GARDINER
table and dessert

LAWRENCE AND COMPANY, LEWISTON
table and dessert

FINEST COMPANY, SOUTH PORTLAND
table and dessert

MARYLAND

MADERA BONDED WINE COMPANY, BALTIMORE
table and dessert, fruit and berry

BOORDY VINEYARD, RIDERWOOD
table

MASSACHUSETTS

GRANADA WINES, CAMBRIDGE
table and dessert, Champagne, brandy, Vermouth

RUBY WINES, EVERETT
table and dessert, fruit wines, Vermouth

SUPREME WINE COMPANY, SOUTH BOSTON
table and dessert, fruit wines, Champagne, sparkling wines, brandy, Vermouth

MICHIGAN

MILAN WINERIES, DETROIT
table and dessert

LA SALLE WINE AND CHAMPAGNE, FARMINGTON
table and dessert, fruit wines, sparkling wines, wine cocktails

MOLLY PITCHER WINES CORPORATION, HARBERT
table and dessert

BRONTE CHAMPAGNE AND WINES COMPANY, HARTFORD
(also Detroit)
table and dessert, Champagne, Vermouth

FRONTENAC WINE COMPANY, PAW PAW (also Detroit)
table and dessert, fruit wines, Champagne, sparkling wines, cocktail wines, Vermouth

MICHIGAN WINERIES, PAW PAW
table and dessert, concentrates

ST. JULIEN WINE COMPANY, PAW PAW
table and dessert, fruit and berry, Champagne, sparkling wines

MISSOURI

AMBROSE AND COMPANY, KANSAS CITY
table and dessert, fruit wines, Champagne, sparkling Burgundy, Vermouth

M. WEPPRICH WINERY, ST. CHARLES
table

BARDENHEIER'S WINE CELLARS, ST. LOUIS
table and dessert, fruit and berry, Champagne, sparkling Burgundy, brandy, Vermouth, special natural wines

NEW JERSEY

GROSS' HIGHLAND WINERY, ABSECON
table and dessert, Champagne, sparkling wines

JACOB LEE WINERY, BORDENTOWN
table

L. N. RENAULT AND SONS
EGG HARBOR CITY
table and dessert, Champagne, sparkling wines, Vermouth

JOHN SCHUSTER AND SON,
EGG HARBOR CITY
table and dessert

TOMASELLO WINERY, HAMMONTON
table and dessert, Champagne, sparkling Burgundy

COAST VINTNERS, JERSEY CITY
dessert

KRUMM'S WINERY, LINWOOD
table and dessert

HERMAN A. KLUXEN WINERY, MADISON
table and dessert, Vermouth, altar wines

LAIRD AND COMPANY, SCOBEYVILLE
table and dessert, brandy

NEW MEXICO

GROSS WINERY, ALBUQUERQUE
table

RICO'S WINERY, ALBUQUERQUE
table

MARCOS GUTIERREZ, SANDOVAL
table

NEW YORK

ROBIN FILS AND CIE, BATAVIA
Champagne, pink Champagne, sparkling Burgundy

EASTERN WINE CORPORATION, BRONX
(also Waterford, California)
table and dessert, fruit wines, Champagne, sparkling wines, Vermouth

GREAT NORTHERN WINE COMPANY,
BRONX
table and dessert, Vermouth

REX WINE CORPORATION, BRONX
table and dessert, Vermouth

THE ROBBINS WINE COMPANY,
BRONX
dessert, fruit wines

MONARCH WINE COMPANY, BROOKLYN
table and dessert, fruit wines, Champagne, Vermouth

MONSIEUR HENRI WINES, BROOKLYN
table and dessert, fruit wines, Champagne, sparkling wines, Vermouth

SAN MARINO WINE CORPORATION,
BROOKLYN
Champagne, sparkling wines

SOLANO WINERY, BROOKLYN
table and dessert, Champagne, sparkling wines, Vermouth

ITALIAN AND FRENCH WINE
COMPANY, BUFFALO
table and dessert, fruit wines, Champagne, sparkling wines, brandy, Vermouth

CANANDAIGUA INDUSTRIES,
CANANDAIGUA
table and dessert, fruit wines, Champagne, kosher wines

MANDIA CHAMPAGNE CELLARS,
CLINTONDALE
table, Champagne, sparkling wines, Vermouth

O-NEH-DA VINEYARDS, CONESUS
altar wines

FREDONIA PRODUCTS COMPANY,
FREDONIA
table and dessert

GOLD SEAL VINEYARDS,
HAMMONDSPORT
table and dessert, Champagne, sparkling Burgundy, sacramental wines

PLEASANT VALLEY WINE COMPANY
(division of Taylor Wine Company),
HAMMONDSPORT
table and dessert, Champagne, sparkling wines, Vermouth

D. W. PUTNAM COMPANY,
HAMMONDSPORT
table and dessert, Champagne, sparkling wines, wine sauce

TAYLOR WINE COMPANY, HAMMONDSPORT
table and dessert, Champagne, Vermouth

HUDSON VALLEY WINE COMPANY,
HIGHLAND
table and dessert, Champagne, sparkling wines, aperitif wines, Vermouth

G. VALENTI WINERY, LAWRENCE, L. I.
table and dessert, fruit wines, Champagne, sparkling wines, Vermouth

CHATEAU GAY, LEWISTON
table, Champagne, sparkling wines

ROYAL WINE CORPORATION, LONG ISLAND CITY
table and dessert, kosher wines, kosher Champagne, wine eggnog, wine jellies

MARLBORO INDUSTRIES, MARLBORO
table, Champagne, sparkling wines, Vermouth

NORTH AMERICA WINES CORPORATION, MASPETH, L. I.
table and dessert, fruit wines, Champagne, kosher wines, Vermouth

WIDMER'S WINE CELLARS, NAPLES
table and dessert, Champagne, sparkling wines, Vermouth

HIGH TOR VINEYARDS, NEW CITY
table

CANNIZZARO WINE COMPANY, NEW YORK
table and dessert, fruit wines, Champagne, Vermouth

GANELES-LENGER WINE CORPORATION, NEW YORK
dessert, fruit wines, kosher wines, honey wine

MONTEREY WINE COMPANY, NEW YORK
table and dessert, fruit wines, Vermouth, Champagne

PURE WINE COMPANY, NEW YORK
table and dessert

SCHAPIRO'S WINE COMPANY, NEW YORK
table and dessert, Vermouth

CAMILLO TESTA, NEW YORK
table and dessert, Champagne, sparkling wines, Vermouth

TRANSAMERICA WINE CORPORATION, NEW YORK
Vermouth

VERMOUTH INDUSTRIES OF AMERICA, NEW YORK
Vermouth

PENN YAN WINE CELLARS, PENN YAN
table and dessert

BROTHERHOOD CORPORATION, WASHINGTONVILLE
table and dessert, Champagne, sparkling wines

DISTILLERIE STOCK U.S.A., WOODSIDE
dessert, Vermouth, brandy

QUALITY FRUIT WINES CORPORATION, YONKERS
table and dessert, fruit and berry

SAN MARTINA WINES, YONKERS
table and dessert, Vermouth

OHIO

ALBERT R. KLINGSHIRN WINERY, AVON LAKE
table

JOHN SCHOBER, AVON LAKE
table and dessert

OHIO WINERY, BEDFORD
table, wine vinegar

CATAWBA ISLAND WINE COMPANY (Mon Ami Champagne Company), CATAWBA ISLAND
table and dessert, sparkling wines

AUGUST ZIMMER WINERY, CINCINNATI
table and dessert, Champagne, sparkling wines

AMERICAN VINEYARDS COMPANY, CLEVELAND
table and dessert, fruit wines, Champagne, sparkling wines

RUDOLPH BOZEGLAV WINERY, CLEVELAND
table and dessert

LOUIS ERSTE, CLEVELAND
table

HAMMER COMPANY, CLEVELAND
table and dessert, Champagne, Vermouth

ANA MARINCIC, CLEVELAND
table and dessert

JULIA MUCHITZ, CLEVELAND
table

POMPEI WINERY, CLEVELAND
table and dessert, fruit wines

RINI WINERY, CLEVELAND
table and dessert, fruit wines, Champagne, Vermouth

JOSEPH J. SMOLE, JR., CLEVELAND
table and dessert

CHRIST JOEHLIN, EAST TOLEDO
table

COHODAS VINEYARDS, GENEVA
table and dessert

LESLIE J. BRETZ, MIDDLE BASS
table, Champagne

GEORGE F. LONZ, MIDDLE BASS
table and dessert, Champagne

EDWARD W. JOHLIN, OREGON
table

HEINEMAN WINERY, PUT-IN-BAY
table and dessert

PUT-IN-BAY WINE COMPANY, PUT-IN-BAY
table and dessert, Champagne, sparkling wines

ENGELS AND KRUDWIG WINE COMPANY, SANDUSKY
table and dessert, Champagne, Vermouth

M. HOMMEL COMPANY, SANDUSKY
Champagne, sparkling wines

STEUK WINE COMPANY, SANDUSKY
table, Champagne, sparkling wines

MEIER'S WINE CELLARS, SILVERTON
(also Cincinnati, George and Sandusky)
table and dessert, fruit wines, Champagne, sparkling wines, Vermouth

MANTEY VINEYARDS, VENICE
table and dessert

CAHOON WINERY, WESTLAKE
table and dessert

DE POLO WINERY, WESTLAKE
table and dessert

DOVER VINEYARDS, WESTLAKE
table and dessert, fruit wines

WICKLIFFE WINERY, WICKLIFFE
table

WILLOUGHBY WINERY, WILLOUGHBY
table

OREGON

FORREST BERRY FARM, BROADBENT
berry wines

HENRY ENDRES WINERY, OREGON CITY
table, loganberry and apple wines

DOERNER'S WINERY, ROSEBURG
table

HONEYWOOD, SALEM
Concord, blackberry, loganberry, currant and cherry wines

PENNSYLVANIA

REINIGER WINE COMPANY, JERMYN
table and dessert, cherry wine

KASSER DISTILLERS PRODUCTS CORPORATION, PHILADELPHIA
table and dessert, fruit wines

JAMES MORONEY, PHILADELPHIA
table and dessert, Champagne, brandy, Vermouth

SPATOLA WINES, PHILADELPHIA
table and dessert, fruit wines, Champagne, Vermouth

WILEN BROTHERS, PHILADELPHIA
table and dessert, fruit wines

SOUTH CAROLINA

TENNER BROTHERS, PATRICK
table and dessert, fruit and berry

TEXAS

VAL VERDE WINERY, DEL RIO
table

VIRGINIA

WOBURN WINERY, CLARKSVILLE
table and dessert

RICHARD'S WINE CELLARS, PETERSBURG
table and dessert

DIXIE WINE COMPANY, RICHMOND
table and dessert, fruit wines

SOUTHLAND WINE COMPANY, RICHMOND
table and dessert, fruit wines

WASHINGTON

ST. CHARLES WINERY, GRAPEVIEW
table and dessert, berry wines

OLD WEST WINES, RENTON
table and dessert, fruit and berry, brandy

AMERICAN WINE GROWERS, SEATTLE
table and dessert, fruit wines

AUBURN WINERIES, SEATTLE
table and dessert, fruit wines

ALHAMBRA WINE COMPANY, SELAH
table and dessert, fruit wines

WERBERGER WINERY AND DISTILLING, SHELTON
table and dessert, fruit wines, loganberry wine

SANTA ROSA WINERY, SUNNYSIDE
table and dessert, fruit and berry, brandy

COLUMBIA WINERIES, VANCOUVER
table and dessert, fruit wines, wine vinegar

WISCONSIN

FRESNO WINE COMPANY, MILWAUKEE
table and dessert, Champagne, sparkling wines, Vermouth, kosher wines

INDEX